Learning Kotlin: Build Android Apps from Scratch

A Complete Guide to Mastering Kotlin for Android Development

MIGUEL FARMER

RAFAEL SANDERS

Table of Content

TABLE OF CONTENTS

INTRODUCTION

Mastering Android Development with Kotlin

Welcome to **"Mastering Android Development with Kotlin"**, a comprehensive guide designed to take you through the entire process of building modern Android applications using Kotlin. Whether you're a beginner just starting out or an experienced developer looking to refine your skills, this book will provide you with the knowledge and tools you need to develop efficient, high-quality Android apps.

Kotlin has quickly become the preferred programming language for Android development, and it's not difficult to see why. With its concise syntax, seamless interoperability with Java, and advanced features like null safety, Kotlin offers developers a robust toolkit for building mobile apps that are not only powerful but also easy to maintain and scale. As of 2017, Google officially endorsed Kotlin as the preferred language for Android development, and since then, Kotlin has seen widespread adoption in the Android developer community.

In this book, we will explore the **Kotlin programming language** in depth, covering everything from basic syntax to advanced features, and how to leverage Kotlin's strengths to build modern, responsive, and efficient Android applications.

What to Expect from This Book

Throughout this book, we will take a hands-on approach to learning, starting with the basics and progressing to advanced concepts. Each chapter is designed to give you a solid understanding of Android development, while incorporating practical examples and real-world scenarios to help you solidify your knowledge.

Key Features of the Book:

- **Step-by-Step Guidance**: Each chapter will guide you through concepts and practical examples, starting with fundamental topics and moving towards more advanced Android development techniques. The goal is to build your knowledge progressively, ensuring you understand both the "how" and the "why" behind Android development with Kotlin.

- **Real-World Projects**: We'll focus on real-world examples and app-building practices. You'll develop fully functional Android apps with each section, which can serve as a foundation for your own personal or professional projects.

- **Practical Code Examples**: The book is packed with code examples designed to show you how to implement features and functionality in Android applications. You will write code alongside us as we break down each component in detail.

- **Kotlin Focus**: As Kotlin is the primary language for Android development, every concept and technique is covered with Kotlin as the central focus. The chapters will emphasize Kotlin's advantages in Android development, including concise syntax, extension functions, null safety, and support for modern paradigms like functional and reactive programming.

Why Kotlin for Android Development?

Kotlin was created with the intent to improve on Java's shortcomings, offering a more streamlined, readable, and maintainable approach to programming. The language introduces a modern, object-oriented and functional programming style, allowing developers to write code that is expressive, easy to understand, and more concise than Java.

Some of the standout features of Kotlin that make it an ideal choice for Android development include:

1. **Concise Syntax**: Kotlin's syntax is more compact than Java, reducing the amount of boilerplate code and making it easier to read and write.

2. **Null Safety**: Kotlin's built-in null safety feature ensures that you are less likely to encounter the infamous **NullPointerException**. This dramatically reduces runtime errors and improves the stability of your apps.

3. **Interoperability with Java**: Kotlin is fully interoperable with Java, meaning you can use existing Java libraries and frameworks without any issues. This allows developers to migrate their Android projects to Kotlin gradually.

4. **Coroutines for Asynchronous Programming**: Kotlin introduces **coroutines**, a powerful way to handle asynchronous tasks like network calls and

background processing in a more efficient and easy-to-read manner.

5. **Modern Features**: Kotlin also supports many modern features, such as **extension functions**, **data classes**, **sealed classes**, and **delegation**, which enhance the expressiveness and maintainability of the code.

What You'll Learn in This Book

We've structured the chapters to provide you with a complete toolkit for building Android applications using Kotlin. Here's a breakdown of what you will learn:

- **Android Basics and Kotlin Fundamentals**: You will begin by learning Kotlin's syntax, basic data types, and object-oriented programming principles. As you get comfortable with the language, we'll introduce you to Android's main components like activities, fragments, views, and layouts.

- **Building and Designing User Interfaces**: This book will take you through various UI components, including buttons, text views, and image views, as well as layouts like **ConstraintLayout** and **RecyclerView**. You will learn how to create fluid, responsive interfaces that work across different devices and screen sizes.

- **Working with Android's Architecture Components**: You will learn to work with **LiveData**, **ViewModels**, and **Room Database** to create a well-structured, maintainable app. We'll also introduce you to **Navigation Components** for managing app navigation with ease.

- **Networking and Firebase**: Building modern apps requires integrating data from external sources. We'll show you how to use **Retrofit** for handling network requests and integrating **Firebase** for features like authentication, real-time databases, and cloud storage.

- **Testing, Debugging, and Optimization**: We'll cover the essential tools and techniques for testing your app's functionality, debugging issues, and optimizing the app's performance. From unit tests to UI testing with Espresso, you'll learn how to ensure your app is stable and performs well.

- **Publishing and Maintaining Apps**: At the end of the book, we will guide you through the process of preparing your app for release, signing it, and uploading it to the **Google Play Store**. We'll also discuss how to maintain and update your app post-release, ensuring that your users continue to have a positive experience.

Who This Book is For

This book is suitable for developers who have some basic programming experience and want to dive into Android development with Kotlin. If you have experience with Java and want to switch to Kotlin for Android development, this book will be an excellent resource to help you transition smoothly.

It is also suitable for those who are already familiar with Android development but want to learn more about modern Android architecture, tools, and techniques that will help them build better, more efficient applications.

If you are a beginner with no prior Android development experience, you may want to take some time to familiarize yourself with basic programming concepts before starting this book. Kotlin's syntax is relatively easy to learn, and you'll be able to pick up the concepts as you progress.

Conclusion

By the end of this book, you will be able to confidently create Android applications using Kotlin, leveraging modern architecture components, performing network operations, managing app data, and optimizing performance. Whether you want to build apps for personal projects or work on enterprise-level solutions, **Mastering Android Development with Kotlin** will provide you with the skills and knowledge needed to succeed.

So, let's dive into Kotlin and Android development, and start building apps that delight users and stand out in the competitive mobile app market. Happy coding!

CHAPTER 1

INTRODUCTION TO KOTLIN AND ANDROID DEVELOPMENT

In this chapter, we'll lay the foundation for your Kotlin journey and dive into Android development, providing all the essential tools you need to get started. We'll also explore why Kotlin is the language of choice for Android development, how to set up your development environment, and the differences between Kotlin and Java in Android development.

Overview of Kotlin

Kotlin is a modern, statically-typed programming language that is fully interoperable with Java. Developed by JetBrains, Kotlin was officially announced as the preferred language for Android development by Google in 2017. It runs on the Java Virtual Machine (JVM) and can be used to write both Android apps and server-side applications.

Kotlin combines simplicity and expressiveness with the power of Java, offering many improvements over Java, such as concise syntax, null safety, and coroutines for asynchronous

15

programming. It's designed to be more readable, less error-prone, and to minimize the boilerplate code that is so common in Java.

Key Features:

- **Concise Syntax**: Reduces the amount of code you need to write.
- **Null Safety**: Helps to eliminate the risk of null pointer exceptions, a common problem in many programming languages.
- **Interoperability**: Kotlin can work alongside Java code in the same project, making the transition to Kotlin smooth for Java developers.
- **Coroutines**: Kotlin's built-in support for asynchronous programming, making background tasks and concurrency easier to manage.

Why Kotlin for Android Development?

Kotlin's rise to prominence in Android development is a result of several key benefits that it brings to the table:

1. **Official Support from Google**: Since Google announced Kotlin as the official language for Android development, the language has been gaining popularity quickly. It's now seen as the preferred language for building modern, high-quality Android apps.

2. **Interoperability with Java**: Many existing Android apps are written in Java. Kotlin offers seamless integration with Java, allowing developers to gradually migrate their codebase to Kotlin. You can mix Kotlin and Java code in the same project, so there's no need for a complete rewrite.

3. **Concise and Readable Code**: Kotlin allows developers to write less code while achieving more. Its syntax is streamlined, reducing the need for boilerplate code, which is especially beneficial for maintaining and updating Android apps.

4. **Null Safety**: One of Kotlin's most popular features is its built-in null safety, which helps prevent common runtime errors such as NullPointerExceptions. This leads to more stable and bug-free applications.

5. **Coroutines for Async Programming**: Kotlin's coroutines simplify asynchronous programming, making background tasks (such as network calls or database queries) much easier to manage compared to Java's thread-based approach.

6. **Strong Android Ecosystem**: Kotlin integrates seamlessly with Android's robust ecosystem of libraries, tools, and frameworks, including Jetpack, which makes Android development faster and more efficient.

7. **Growing Community and Resources**: Kotlin has a strong, growing community of developers, making it easier to find resources, libraries, and solutions to

common problems. Google, JetBrains, and other companies provide official support, ensuring Kotlin remains up-to-date with Android's evolving needs.

Setting Up Your Development Environment (Android Studio, SDK, etc.)

Before you begin writing Kotlin code for Android, you need to set up your development environment. Android Studio is the official Integrated Development Environment (IDE) for Android development, and it supports Kotlin out of the box. Here's how you can get started:

1. **Install Android Studio**:
    o   Download and install Android Studio from the official website.
    o   Follow the installation instructions for your operating system (Windows, macOS, or Linux).
    o   During installation, Android Studio will also install the necessary Android SDK components.

2. **Set Up the SDK**:
    o   Once Android Studio is installed, it will prompt you to download the Android SDK (Software Development Kit), which is a collection of tools and libraries required for Android development.

o   Make sure to install the required SDK packages and tools, such as the latest Android API levels, build tools, and emulator images.

3.   **Create a New Kotlin Project**:

o   Launch Android Studio and select "Start a new Android Studio project."

o   Choose a project template (e.g., Empty Activity) and make sure that the "Language" option is set to Kotlin.

o   Android Studio will automatically configure the project to use Kotlin, including adding necessary Kotlin dependencies to your build.gradle files.

4.   **Set Up Emulators for Testing**:

o   Android Studio allows you to test your Android app on virtual devices (emulators). You can set up different device configurations to simulate phones, tablets, or other Android devices.

o   To set up an emulator, navigate to **Tools > AVD Manager** and create a new Android Virtual Device (AVD) with your desired specifications.

5.   **Syncing with Gradle**:

o   Gradle is the build automation tool used by Android Studio. After setting up your project, Android Studio will automatically sync the Gradle files. This allows you to download and manage project dependencies, build configurations, and settings.

The Kotlin Syntax vs Java for Android Development

While Kotlin and Java both target the JVM and are used in Android development, Kotlin offers many advantages over Java in terms of syntax, conciseness, and safety.

1. **Conciseness**:
   - **Kotlin**: Kotlin requires fewer lines of code. For example, setting up a simple `TextView` in Kotlin is much more compact compared to Java.
   - **Java**: Java's syntax tends to be more verbose, requiring extra lines of code for basic tasks that Kotlin handles more succinctly.

Example:

   - Kotlin:

```kotlin
val textView: TextView = findViewById(R.id.textView)
textView.text = "Hello Kotlin"
```

   - Java:

20

```java
java

TextView          textView          =
findViewById(R.id.textView);
textView.setText("Hello Java");
```

2. **Null Safety**:

   o **Kotlin**: One of the key features of Kotlin is its null safety. Kotlin enforces safe handling of nullable types, reducing the chances of NullPointerExceptions at runtime.

   o **Java**: Java allows null references, leading to potential NullPointerExceptions unless handled explicitly.

3. **Data Classes**:

   o **Kotlin**: Kotlin introduces `data class`, which automatically generates `toString()`, `equals()`, `hashCode()`, and `()` methods, making it easier to work with data objects.

   o **Java**: Java requires developers to manually write `getters`, `setters`, `toString()`, and `equals()` methods.

   Example:

   o Kotlin:

```kotlin
kotlin
```

21

```
data class User(val name: String, val
age: Int)
```

o   Java:

```java
public class User {
    private String name;
    private int age;
    // Getters and setters
}
```

4. **Lambdas and Higher-Order Functions**:

   o   **Kotlin**: Kotlin supports functional programming features like lambda expressions, which make working with collections, UI elements, and asynchronous tasks much easier.

   o   **Java**: Java introduced lambdas in Java 8, but they are less concise and flexible compared to Kotlin.

5. **Extension Functions**:

   o   **Kotlin**: You can extend existing classes with new functionality without modifying their code using extension functions.

   o   **Java**: Java does not support extension functions natively. Any new functionality must be added through inheritance or composition.

22

In the next chapters, we'll delve deeper into Kotlin's syntax, its unique features, and how to start building real Android apps using this modern language. By the end of this book, you'll have all the tools you need to create powerful, scalable Android applications with Kotlin.

CHAPTER 2

YOUR FIRST KOTLIN PROGRAM

Now that you've learned about Kotlin and Android development, it's time to dive into your first Kotlin program. This chapter will guide you through setting up a simple Kotlin project, understanding Kotlin's structure, writing your first "Hello World" program, and exploring some fundamental Kotlin concepts like variables, types, and functions.

Setting Up a Simple Kotlin Project

To start building with Kotlin, you'll need to create a Kotlin project. Android Studio makes this process seamless, especially since it now fully supports Kotlin.

Steps for Setting Up a Kotlin Project:

1. **Open Android Studio**:
   - o If you haven't already, launch Android Studio. Make sure you have it installed along with the necessary SDK and emulator as described in Chapter 1.

2. **Create a New Project**:

- o From the Android Studio welcome screen, click on **"Start a New Android Studio Project"**.
- o Select the **"Empty Activity"** template for simplicity.
- o In the **"Language"** dropdown, select **Kotlin** (this is the default now, so it will likely be pre-selected).
- o Set the **name** of your project (e.g., "HelloKotlin") and specify your desired project location.
- o Click **Finish** to create your project.

3. **Explore the Project Files**:
   - o After your project is created, you'll see a file structure similar to this:
     - **MainActivity.kt** (your main Kotlin file for the app's entry point)
     - **activity_main.xml** (the layout file where you define the UI)
   - o For this exercise, you'll focus on modifying the **MainActivity.kt** file to display your "Hello World" message.

Understanding Kotlin's Structure

Before writing your first program, let's break down the structure of a simple Kotlin program and understand its components.

In Kotlin, every application has an **entry point**, which is a function called `main`. This function is where the program begins execution. The basic structure of a Kotlin program looks like this:

```kotlin

fun main() {
    println("Hello, Kotlin!")
}
```

- **fun main()**: This is the entry point of a Kotlin application. The `fun` keyword is used to define a function, and `main` is the name of the function.
- **println("Hello, Kotlin!")**: This line prints the text "Hello, Kotlin!" to the console. `println()` is a built-in function in Kotlin used for output.

Writing Your First "Hello World" Program

Now that you understand the basics, let's write your first Kotlin program!

1. Open your **MainActivity.kt** file.
2. Inside the `onCreate` method (where the app's UI elements are typically initialized), you can add a print statement to display your message in the log.

26

Here's how you could set up your first Kotlin program:

```kotlin
package com.example.hellokotlin

import android.os.Bundle
import androidx.appcompat.app.AppCompatActivity
import android.util.Log

class MainActivity : AppCompatActivity() {

    override fun onCreate(savedInstanceState: Bundle?) {
        super.onCreate(savedInstanceState)
        setContentView(R.layout.activity_main)

        // This is where you print "Hello, Kotlin!" in the Android Log
        Log.d("MainActivity", "Hello, Kotlin!")
    }
}
```

Explanation:

- **package com.example.hellokotlin**: Defines the package of the Kotlin file, which helps organize the code.
- **import android.os.Bundle**: Imports necessary Android classes.

- **`class MainActivity : AppCompatActivity()`**: Defines the `MainActivity` class, inheriting from `AppCompatActivity`, which provides the basic functionality for Android activities.

- **`override fun onCreate(savedInstanceState: Bundle?)`**: The `onCreate` method is where the activity initializes, including setting the content view and performing any setup required.

- **`Log.d("MainActivity", "Hello, Kotlin!")`**: This line logs the message "Hello, Kotlin!" to Android's Logcat, which you can view in Android Studio's Logcat window. This is helpful for debugging and confirming that the program runs successfully.

Explanation of Basic Kotlin Concepts (Variables, Types, and Functions)

Before diving deeper into Android development, it's crucial to understand a few basic Kotlin concepts like variables, types, and functions. These are fundamental to writing efficient and readable Kotlin code.

1. **Variables in Kotlin**: In Kotlin, you define variables using two keywords: `val` and `var`.
   - **`val`** (immutable variable): A value assigned to a `val` cannot be changed after initialization.

28

```kotlin
kotlin

val greeting = "Hello, Kotlin!" //
This cannot be reassigned later
```

- o **var** (mutable variable): A value assigned to a var can be changed.

```kotlin
kotlin

var counter = 10
counter = 15 // This is allowed
```

2. **Types in Kotlin**: Kotlin is statically typed, which means that the type of a variable is known at compile time. The most common types are:
    - o **Primitive Types**: Int, Double, Float, Boolean, Char
    - o **String**: A sequence of characters.

```kotlin
kotlin

val number: Int = 10
val temperature: Double = 36.6
val isActive: Boolean = true
val letter: Char = 'A'
val name: String = "Kotlin"
```

3. Kotlin also supports **nullable types** using `?`. This means a variable can either hold a value or be null:

4. `kotlin`

5.

6. `val name: String? = null // This can be null`

7. **Functions in Kotlin**: Functions in Kotlin are defined using the `fun` keyword. Functions can accept parameters and return values.

   o **Basic Function**:

   ```kotlin
   fun greet() {
       println("Hello, Kotlin!")
   }
   ```

   o **Function with Parameters**:

   ```kotlin
   fun greet(name: String) {
       println("Hello, $name!")
   }
   ```

   o **Function with Return Value**:

   ```kotlin
   ```

30

```
fun sum(a: Int, b: Int): Int {
    return a + b
}
```

Calling the function:

```
kotlin


val result = sum(5, 10)
println("The sum is: $result")
```

o **Expression Body Function**: Kotlin allows you to
   define a function with a single expression using
   the expression body syntax.

```
kotlin


fun multiply(a: Int, b: Int) = a * b
```

Key Takeaways

- You've set up your first Kotlin project and written a
  simple "Hello World" program that outputs to Logcat.
- Kotlin offers a concise, expressive syntax that is
  beginner-friendly yet powerful.
- You've learned the basics of variables, data types, and
  functions in Kotlin, which form the building blocks of
  every Android app.

31

In the next chapters, we'll build on these basics, gradually diving into more advanced Kotlin concepts and Android development techniques.

CHAPTER 3

UNDERSTANDING ANDROID DEVELOPMENT BASICS

In this chapter, we'll explore the essential aspects of Android development. You'll learn what Android is, get an overview of Android Studio, understand the core components of Android apps, and see how Kotlin fits into the Android development ecosystem. This foundation will prepare you for building your first Android app using Kotlin.

What is Android?

Android is an open-source operating system for mobile devices, primarily smartphones and tablets. Developed by Google, it's based on the Linux kernel and is designed to be flexible, scalable, and user-friendly. Android allows developers to create powerful, feature-rich mobile applications for a wide range of devices.

Key Points about Android:

- **Open Source**: Android is an open-source project, meaning anyone can access its source code and contribute to its development.

- **Wide Device Range**: Android runs on a wide variety of devices, including smartphones, tablets, smart TVs, wearables, and even cars.
- **Application Framework**: Android provides a rich application framework that allows developers to create interactive, high-performance applications.
- **Global Reach**: With millions of active users worldwide, Android dominates the global smartphone market, making it an essential platform for developers.

Android applications are written in Java, Kotlin, or C++, and they use various libraries and frameworks to interact with Android's core features.

Android Studio Overview

Android Studio is the official IDE (Integrated Development Environment) for Android development. It's built on IntelliJ IDEA and provides all the tools needed to develop, test, and debug Android apps.

Key Features of Android Studio:

- **Code Editor**: Android Studio comes with a powerful code editor that supports Kotlin, Java, and other languages. It provides syntax highlighting, code suggestions, refactoring tools, and more.

- **Layout Editor**: Android Studio includes a visual layout editor that allows developers to drag and drop UI elements (e.g., buttons, text fields) to design their app's interface.

- **Android Emulator**: The emulator lets you run your app on a virtual device, so you can test it without needing a physical device.

- **Integrated Debugging Tools**: Android Studio includes advanced debugging tools, such as Logcat, to help you track app behavior and fix issues in real-time.

- **Gradle Support**: Android Studio uses Gradle as the build system, allowing you to automate tasks like building and packaging your app. Gradle handles dependencies and optimizes the build process.

- **Performance and Profiling Tools**: Android Studio offers tools to monitor and optimize your app's performance, including memory usage, CPU usage, and network traffic.

The Android App Architecture: Activities, Views, Layouts, and Intents

Understanding the basic building blocks of an Android app is key to developing robust applications. Here are the primary components of Android architecture:

1. **Activities**:

- o An **Activity** represents a single screen in an Android app. It's where most of your app's logic and UI elements live.
- o Each Android app starts with a main activity (e.g., MainActivity). Activities handle the user interface and interaction, and they manage the flow of your app.
- o The onCreate() method is the entry point for initializing the activity when it's launched.

Example: In the MainActivity, you might initialize UI elements like buttons and text views, and set up event listeners.

kotlin

```
class MainActivity : AppCompatActivity() {
    override                          fun
onCreate(savedInstanceState: Bundle?) {

super.onCreate(savedInstanceState)

setContentView(R.layout.activity_main)
    }
}
```

2. **Views**:

- o Views are UI elements that users interact with in an Android app. Examples of views include buttons, text fields, checkboxes, and images.
- o Each view is an instance of a specific class (e.g., `Button`, `TextView`, `ImageView`), and you can customize their properties to match your app's design.
- o Views are typically added to layouts, which define the structure and arrangement of the views.

3. **Layouts**:

- o A **Layout** defines how the views are arranged on the screen. Layouts can be simple (e.g., a `LinearLayout` where views are stacked vertically or horizontally) or complex (e.g., `ConstraintLayout`).
- o Layouts are defined in XML files (e.g., `activity_main.xml`), where you specify the positioning and size of views.

Example: A simple layout with a button and a text view.

xml

```
<LinearLayout
xmlns:android="http://schemas.android.com
/apk/res/android"
    android:layout_width="match_parent"
```

```xml
        android:layout_height="match_parent"
        android:orientation="vertical">

    <Button
        android:id="@+id/button"

    android:layout_width="wrap_content"

    android:layout_height="wrap_content"
        android:text="Click Me" />

    <TextView
        android:id="@+id/textView"

    android:layout_width="wrap_content"

    android:layout_height="wrap_content"
        android:text="Hello World" />
</LinearLayout>
```

4. **Intents**:

   - An **Intent** is a messaging object that facilitates communication between components in an Android app. Intents are used to start activities, send broadcasts, or interact with services.
   - For example, you can use an intent to navigate from one activity to another or to open a website in a browser.

38

Example: Starting a new activity using an intent.

```kotlin
val intent = Intent(this,
SecondActivity::class.java)
startActivity(intent)
```

Intents can also pass data between activities. For example, passing a string from one activity to another:

```kotlin
val intent = Intent(this,
SecondActivity::class.java)
intent.putExtra("EXTRA_MESSAGE", "Hello,
Kotlin!")
startActivity(intent)
```

In the receiving activity:

```kotlin
val message =
intent.getStringExtra("EXTRA_MESSAGE")
textView.text = message
```

How Kotlin Integrates with Android

Kotlin seamlessly integrates with Android, allowing developers to write modern, concise, and safe code for Android apps.

1. **Android Studio Support**: Android Studio fully supports Kotlin, making it the preferred language for Android development. When creating a new project, Kotlin is set as the default language, but Java is also supported for legacy apps.

2. **Kotlin Extensions**: Kotlin offers several useful extensions for Android development. For example, you can use Kotlin's synthetic properties to access views directly, instead of calling `findViewById()`.

Before Kotlin Extensions:

```kotlin
```

```kotlin
val      textView:      TextView      =
findViewById(R.id.textView)
```

With Kotlin Extensions:

```kotlin
```

```kotlin
textView.text = "Hello Kotlin"
```

(Note: Kotlin synthetic properties are deprecated in recent versions of Android. The recommended approach now is to use `ViewBinding` or `DataBinding`.)

3. **Null Safety**: Kotlin's built-in null safety makes handling `NullPointerExceptions` much easier, which is a common problem in Android development. In Kotlin, you can declare nullable types with the `?` operator, which ensures that null values are handled explicitly.

Example:

```kotlin

val name: String? = null
println(name?.length)    //    Prints    null
without causing a crash
```

4. **Coroutines**: Kotlin's coroutines are widely used for managing background tasks and asynchronous programming in Android. Coroutines allow you to run background tasks like network requests or database operations without blocking the main UI thread, providing a smooth user experience.

Example:

```kotlin

```

41

```
GlobalScope.launch(Dispatchers.Main) {
    val result = fetchDataFromNetwork() //
Suspend function
    textView.text = result
}
```

Key Takeaways

- **Android** is an open-source operating system that allows developers to create apps for smartphones, tablets, and other devices.
- **Android Studio** is the official IDE for Android development, with built-in support for Kotlin, an intuitive UI editor, and debugging tools.
- The basic **Android architecture** consists of components like Activities, Views, Layouts, and Intents, which are used to build interactive apps.
- **Kotlin** integrates smoothly with Android, offering advantages like null safety, concise syntax, and support for modern features like coroutines and extension functions.

In the next chapters, we'll explore how to build a real Android app using Kotlin, utilizing the core concepts you've learned in this chapter.

CHAPTER 4

KOTLIN DATA TYPES AND VARIABLES

In this chapter, we'll explore how Kotlin handles data types and variables. We'll discuss the different types of variables and constants, how Kotlin handles primitive types versus object types, nullable types and how to ensure null safety, and Kotlin's powerful type inference system. Understanding these concepts is crucial for writing clean and efficient Kotlin code in Android development.

Variables and Constants

In Kotlin, variables and constants are declared using the `var` and `val` keywords, respectively.

- **`var` (Mutable Variables)**: The `var` keyword is used to declare a variable whose value can be changed during the program's execution.

  Example:

  ```kotlin
  kotlin
  ```

```
var age: Int = 25
age = 30  // The value can be modified
```

In this example, `age` is a mutable variable that can be reassigned.

- **val (Immutable Variables or Constants)**: The `val` keyword is used to declare a constant. Once a value is assigned to a `val` variable, it cannot be reassigned.

Example:

```kotlin
val name: String = "John"
// name = "Doe"  // This would cause an error because `name` is a constant
```

In this case, `name` is an immutable variable (constant) that cannot be reassigned after initialization.

Both `val` and `var` can be used to declare variables for any data type in Kotlin, but `val` ensures immutability, which is useful for preventing accidental changes to critical data.

Primitive Types vs. Object Types

Kotlin is a statically typed language, meaning that all variables must have a type specified either explicitly or inferred by the compiler. Kotlin distinguishes between **primitive types** and **object types**.

1. **Primitive Types**: In Kotlin, the primitive types are similar to those in Java, such as `Int`, `Double`, `Float`, `Char`, and `Boolean`. However, unlike Java, Kotlin doesn't use primitive wrappers for primitive types — they are treated as regular objects.

   Common Primitive Types in Kotlin:

   o `Int`: Integer values.

   o `Double`: Floating-point numbers.

   o `Float`: Floating-point numbers (single precision).

   o `Boolean`: Logical values, `true` or `false`.

   o `Char`: A single character.

   Example:

   ```kotlin
   val number: Int = 42
   val pi: Double = 3.14159
   ```

```kotlin
val isKotlinFun: Boolean = true
val letter: Char = 'K'
```

These primitive types are automatically optimized by the Kotlin compiler, meaning that they are efficiently handled in memory, just like in Java.

2. **Object Types**: Object types in Kotlin are used for more complex structures. They include data types like String, List, Map, and custom classes. Kotlin treats all non-primitive types as objects, meaning they have methods and properties attached to them.

Example:

```kotlin
kotlin

val greeting: String = "Hello, Kotlin!"
val list: List<Int> = listOf(1, 2, 3, 4, 5)
```

Kotlin uses its type system to seamlessly handle primitive and object types. For example, an Int is represented as an object when you need to call methods on it, but it behaves as a primitive type in operations for performance reasons.

Nullable Types and Null Safety

One of Kotlin's most significant features is its handling of null safety. In many programming languages, null values can cause runtime exceptions like the dreaded `NullPointerException`. Kotlin provides robust null safety to help you avoid these issues.

1. **Nullable Types**: In Kotlin, you can declare a variable as nullable by appending a `?` to the type. This means the variable can either hold a value of the specified type or be `null`.

   Example:

   ```kotlin
   val name: String? = null  // This variable
   can hold a String or null
   ```

   In this example, `name` is a nullable string, meaning it can either be a string or `null`.

2. **Null Safety Operators**: Kotlin provides several operators to safely handle nullable types.
   - **Safe Call (?.)**: The safe call operator allows you to access properties or call methods on nullable types safely. If the object is `null`, the operation

47

will return `null` instead of throwing an exception.

Example:

```kotlin
val length: Int? = name?.length  // If name is null, length will be null, not an exception
```

o **Elvis Operator (?:)**: The Elvis operator provides a default value in case a nullable expression evaluates to `null`.

Example:

```kotlin
val length: Int = name?.length ?: 0 // If name is null, length will be set to 0
```

o **Non-null Assertion (!!)**: If you are sure that a nullable variable is not `null`, you can use the non-null assertion operator (`!!`). However, be cautious because if the variable is `null`, it will throw a `NullPointerException`.

Example:

```kotlin
val length: Int = name!!.length  //
Throws an exception if name is null
```

3. By using these operators, Kotlin allows you to handle nullable types in a safe and efficient manner.

Type Inference in Kotlin

Kotlin is designed to be expressive while keeping the code concise. One of the features that help achieve this is **type inference**. Type inference means that Kotlin can automatically determine the type of a variable based on its value, so you don't always need to explicitly specify the type.

- **Basic Type Inference**: Kotlin can infer the type of a variable from its initializer. You can omit the type declaration entirely, and Kotlin will figure it out.

Example:

```kotlin
val age = 25  // Kotlin infers the type to
be Int
```

```
val name = "John"   // Kotlin infers the
type to be String
```

In this example, `age` is inferred as an `Int` and `name` as a `String`, based on the assigned values.

- **When Explicit Type Declaration is Needed**: You'll still need to explicitly declare the type when it's not clear or when the type cannot be inferred.

Example:

```
kotlin
```

```
val list: List<Int> = listOf(1, 2, 3)  //
Here, the type is explicitly declared
```

While Kotlin's type inference is powerful, explicitly declaring types is still common in more complex scenarios, such as with generics or when the type cannot be inferred with certainty.

Key Takeaways

- **Variables and Constants**: Use `var` for mutable variables and `val` for constants (immutable variables).

- **Primitive Types vs. Object Types**: Kotlin treats primitive types (like `Int`, `Boolean`, etc.) as both primitive and object types, optimizing for performance while enabling object-like behavior when necessary.

- **Nullable Types and Null Safety**: Kotlin ensures null safety with nullable types, safe call operators, the Elvis operator, and the non-null assertion operator, making it easy to work with `null` without risking exceptions.

- **Type Inference**: Kotlin can automatically infer the type of a variable from its initializer, reducing the need for explicit type declarations, but you can still specify types when necessary.

In the next chapters, we'll build on these data types and variable concepts as we dive into more advanced Kotlin programming techniques for Android app development.

CHAPTER 5

FUNCTIONS IN KOTLIN

In this chapter, we'll dive into one of the most important aspects of Kotlin programming: functions. Functions are a fundamental part of programming, allowing you to define reusable blocks of code that can take inputs and return outputs. We'll cover how to define functions, handle function parameters and return types, work with lambda expressions and higher-order functions, and explore function overloading and default arguments.

Defining Functions

In Kotlin, functions are defined using the `fun` keyword. A function can take zero or more parameters and can either return a value or be `Unit` (the equivalent of `void` in other languages).

Basic Function Definition:

```kotlin

fun greet() {
    println("Hello, Kotlin!")
}
```

In this simple function:

- `fun` is the keyword used to define the function.
- `greet` is the function name.
- The function has no parameters and does not return any value (implicitly `Unit`).

Function with Parameters and Return Value: You can define functions that take parameters and return a result. The type of each parameter is specified after the parameter name, and the return type is indicated after a colon :.

kotlin

```kotlin
fun sum(a: Int, b: Int): Int {
    return a + b
}
```

Here, `sum` takes two `Int` parameters and returns an `Int` result.

Calling Functions: Once a function is defined, you can call it using its name and passing any required parameters.

kotlin

```kotlin
val result = sum(5, 10)  // Calls the function
sum() and returns 15
println(result)  // Prints: 15
```

1. **Parameter Types**: Each parameter in a function must have a type specified, whether it's a basic type (like `Int` or `String`) or a more complex type (like a custom class or a list).

Example:

```kotlin
fun multiply(x: Double, y: Double): Double
{
    return x * y
}
```

2. **Return Types**: The return type of a function is specified after the colon : in the function signature. If a function doesn't return anything, you can specify `Unit` as the return type, but in most cases, this is omitted because it's the default.

Example with Unit:

```kotlin
fun printMessage(message: String): Unit {
    println(message)
}
```

Here, the function doesn't return anything, so we use `Unit`, which is Kotlin's equivalent of `void`. However, you can leave it out and Kotlin will assume `Unit` by default.

Example with Return Type:

kotlin

```
fun add(a: Int, b: Int): Int {
    return a + b
}
```

3. **Default Return Value**: If the function doesn't explicitly return a value, it implicitly returns `Unit` (void). You can make the return type optional if you intend to return nothing.

Lambda Expressions and Higher-Order Functions

1. **Lambda Expressions**: Kotlin supports **lambda expressions**, which are anonymous functions that can be passed as arguments to functions. Lambdas allow you to define function-like behavior on the fly.

Syntax for Lambda Expressions:

kotlin

```kotlin
val addNumbers = { a: Int, b: Int -> a + b
}
println(addNumbers(5, 3))  // Output: 8
```

In this example:

- o `val addNumbers` is a variable that holds a lambda expression.
- o `{ a: Int, b: Int -> a + b }` is the lambda body that takes two parameters and returns their sum.

You can pass this lambda function to other functions or use it directly.

2. **Higher-Order Functions**: A **higher-order function** is a function that takes one or more functions as parameters or returns a function. In Kotlin, functions can be passed as arguments, enabling functional programming patterns.

   Example of Higher-Order Function:

   ```
   kotlin
   ```

   ```kotlin
   fun calculate(a: Int, b: Int, operation:
   (Int, Int) -> Int): Int {
       return operation(a, b)
   }
   ```

The `calculate` function takes two integers and a function `operation` that accepts two integers and returns an integer. You can pass different operations to this function, making it flexible.

Example of Calling a Higher-Order Function:

```kotlin
val sumResult = calculate(5, 3) { x, y ->
x + y }
val multiplyResult = calculate(5, 3) { x,
y -> x * y }

println("Sum: $sumResult")  // Output: Sum:
8
println("Product: $multiplyResult")    //
Output: Product: 15
```

Here, `calculate` is passed a lambda function that performs different operations based on what's required.

Function Overloading and Default Arguments

1. **Function Overloading**: **Function overloading** allows you to define multiple functions with the same name but different parameter types or numbers. This is useful for

handling various types of input with the same function name.

Example of Function Overloading:

```kotlin

fun greet(name: String) {
    println("Hello, $name!")
}

fun greet() {
    println("Hello, guest!")
}
```

Here, we have two `greet` functions:

- o One takes a `String` parameter (`name`).
- o The other doesn't take any parameters.

Kotlin will determine which function to call based on the number and type of arguments passed.

Calling Overloaded Functions:

```kotlin

greet("Alice")  // Calls the function with a String argument
```

```
greet()    // Calls the function with no
arguments
```

2. **Default Arguments**: Kotlin allows you to define **default argument values** in your functions. This feature allows you to call a function without passing certain arguments, and the default values will be used instead.

Example of Default Arguments:

```kotlin
fun greet(name: String = "Guest", age: Int
= 30) {
    println("Hello, $name! You are $age
years old.")
}
```

In this example, the `name` and `age` parameters have default values. If you call `greet()` without arguments, the function will use the default values.

Calling Functions with Default Arguments:

```kotlin
greet()    // Uses default values: "Hello,
Guest! You are 30 years old."
```

```
greet("John")  // Uses default age: "Hello,
John! You are 30 years old."
greet("Alice", 25)    // Uses provided
values: "Hello, Alice! You are 25 years
old."
```

Default arguments allow for more flexible function calls and cleaner code, especially when there are many optional parameters.

Key Takeaways

- **Defining Functions**: Functions in Kotlin are defined using the `fun` keyword. They can take parameters, return values, and be called with different arguments.
- **Function Parameters and Return Types**: You define the parameters and return types using the : syntax, and you can use `Unit` for functions that don't return anything.
- **Lambda Expressions**: Kotlin supports lambda expressions, which are anonymous functions that can be passed as arguments to other functions.
- **Higher-Order Functions**: Kotlin allows higher-order functions, which can accept functions as parameters or return them as results.
- **Function Overloading and Default Arguments**: You can define multiple functions with the same name but

different parameters (overloading) and provide default values for function parameters, making your code more flexible.

In the next chapters, we'll continue building on these function concepts as we dive into more advanced Kotlin programming techniques and Android app development.

CHAPTER 6

OBJECT-ORIENTED PROGRAMMING IN KOTLIN

In this chapter, we'll explore the key concepts of Object-Oriented Programming (OOP) in Kotlin. OOP is a programming paradigm based on the concept of "objects", which can contain data in the form of fields (properties) and code in the form of methods (functions). Kotlin is fully object-oriented, and understanding the fundamentals of classes, objects, inheritance, and visibility modifiers is essential for building robust and scalable applications.

Classes and Objects

In Kotlin, **classes** are the templates for creating objects. An **object** is an instance of a class, and it can hold properties and methods defined in the class.

1. **Defining a Class**: A class is defined using the `class` keyword. It can contain properties (variables) and methods (functions) that define its behavior.

   Example:

```kotlin
class Person(val name: String, val age:
Int) {
    fun greet() {
        println("Hello, my name is $name
and I am $age years old.")
    }
}
```

In this example:

- o Person is the class name.
- o name and age are properties of the class.
- o The greet function is a method that prints a greeting message.

2. **Creating an Object (Instance of a Class)**: To create an object, you simply use the class name followed by parentheses.

Example:

```kotlin
val person = Person("Alice", 30)
person.greet()   // Output: Hello, my name
is Alice and I am 30 years old.
```

In this example, we created an object of the `Person` class named `person` and called the `greet` method.

Constructors and Initialization

Kotlin allows you to define constructors in two ways: **primary constructors** and **secondary constructors**.

1. **Primary Constructor**: The **primary constructor** is part of the class header and is used to initialize properties directly when an object is created.

    Example:

    ```kotlin
    class Person(val name: String, val age: Int) {
        fun greet() {
            println("Hello, my name is $name and I am $age years old.")
        }
    }
    ```

    Here, `name` and `age` are defined in the primary constructor, and Kotlin automatically generates the code to initialize them when the `Person` object is created.

2. **Secondary Constructor**: A **secondary constructor** is used when you need more complex initialization logic, or you need multiple ways to create an object.

Example:

```kotlin
class Person(val name: String, val age:
Int) {
    constructor(name: String) : this(name,
0) {
        println("This person's age is
unknown.")
    }
    fun greet() {
        println("Hello, my name is $name
and I am $age years old.")
    }
}

val person1 = Person("Alice", 30)
val person2 = Person("Bob")   // Uses the
secondary constructor
```

- o The secondary constructor allows you to create a Person with just a name, and it defaults the age to 0.

○ The : `this()` syntax calls the primary constructor.

3. **Initializing Properties**: You can also initialize properties with default values directly in the class body or by using `init` blocks.

Example:

```kotlin
class Person(val name: String) {
    val greeting: String

    init {
        greeting = "Hello, my name is $name"
    }
}

val person = Person("Alice")
println(person.greeting)    // Output: Hello, my name is Alice
```

○ The `init` block is executed when the object is created and can be used to initialize properties or perform setup tasks.

66

Inheritance, Interfaces, and Abstract Classes

1. **Inheritance**: Kotlin supports **single inheritance**, meaning that a class can inherit from another class to reuse properties and methods.

   o A class is **inherited** by using the `:` `ClassName()` syntax.

   o The base class must be marked as `open` to allow other classes to inherit from it.

Example:

```kotlin
kotlin

open class Animal(val name: String) {
    fun speak() {
        println("I am an animal.")
    }
}

class Dog(name: String) : Animal(name) {
    fun bark() {
        println("Woof!")
    }
}

val dog = Dog("Rex")
dog.speak()  // Output: I am an animal.
dog.bark()   // Output: Woof!
```

In this example:

- o `Animal` is the base class, and it is marked with the `open` keyword so that other classes can inherit from it.
- o `Dog` is a subclass that inherits from `Animal` and adds its own method, `bark()`.

2. **Interfaces**: An **interface** is a contract that defines methods that can be implemented by classes. Kotlin allows classes to implement multiple interfaces, unlike single inheritance.

Example:

kotlin

```
interface Swimmable {
    fun swim()
}

class Fish : Swimmable {
    override fun swim() {
        println("The fish is swimming.")
    }
}

val fish = Fish()
fish.swim()    // Output: The fish is
swimming.
```

- o The `Swimmable` interface defines a `swim()` method.
- o The `Fish` class implements the `Swimmable` interface and provides its own implementation of the `swim()` method.

3. **Abstract Classes**: An **abstract class** is a class that cannot be instantiated on its own. It is designed to be subclassed by other classes. Abstract classes can have abstract methods (methods without implementation) as well as concrete methods (methods with implementation).

Example:

```kotlin
abstract class Animal {
    abstract fun makeSound()

    fun sleep() {
        println("The animal is sleeping.")
    }
}

class Dog : Animal() {
    override fun makeSound() {
        println("Woof!")
    }
}
```

69

```
val dog = Dog()
dog.makeSound()   // Output: Woof!
dog.sleep()       // Output: The animal is
sleeping.
```

- o The `Animal` class is abstract and cannot be instantiated directly. It defines an abstract method `makeSound()`, which must be overridden by any subclass.
- o The `Dog` class inherits from `Animal` and provides an implementation for the `makeSound()` method.

Visibility Modifiers (Private, Public, Protected)

Kotlin provides various **visibility modifiers** that control the accessibility of classes, methods, and properties. The most common visibility modifiers are:

1. **public**:
   - o The default visibility modifier for classes, methods, and properties.
   - o The member is visible to all classes everywhere.

Example:

70

```
kotlin

class Person {
    public val name: String = "Alice"
}
```

2. **private**:
   - o The member is visible only within the class or file where it is defined.
   - o Used to encapsulate functionality that should not be accessible from outside the class.

Example:

```
kotlin

class Person {
    private val age: Int = 30    // Only accessible within the Person class
}
```

3. **protected**:
   - o The member is visible within the class and its subclasses, but not from outside.

Example:

```
kotlin
```

71

```
open class Animal {
    protected  val  species:  String  =
"Unknown"
}

class Dog : Animal() {
    fun printSpecies() {
        println(species)    // Accessible
within the subclass
    }
}
```

In this case, `species` is accessible within `Animal` and `Dog` but not from other classes.

4. **internal**:
   o The member is visible only within the same module (a module is a collection of files compiled together).

Key Takeaways

- **Classes and Objects**: Kotlin uses classes to define blueprints for objects. An object is an instance of a class, which can have properties and methods.
- **Constructors and Initialization**: Kotlin supports primary and secondary constructors for initializing

objects, along with the `init` block for complex initialization.

- **Inheritance, Interfaces, and Abstract Classes**: Kotlin supports inheritance (single inheritance), interfaces (multiple inheritance), and abstract classes for reusable code and defining contracts.

- **Visibility Modifiers**: Kotlin uses visibility modifiers (`public`, `private`, `protected`, `internal`) to control access to classes, methods, and properties.

In the next chapters, we'll continue building on these OOP concepts as we delve into more advanced features and techniques in Kotlin and Android development.

CHAPTER 7

WORKING WITH COLLECTIONS
IN KOTLIN

In this chapter, we'll explore Kotlin's powerful **collections framework**. Collections are essential for storing and manipulating data in your application. Kotlin provides a range of collection types such as **Lists**, **Sets**, and **Maps**, each serving a different purpose. We'll cover how to create, modify, and iterate over these collections, and how to filter, transform, and sort the data within them. Additionally, we'll explore how Kotlin handles nullability within collections, making it safer and easier to work with.

Lists, Sets, and Maps

Kotlin has three main types of collections: **Lists**, **Sets**, and **Maps**. Each of these has specific characteristics and use cases.

1. **Lists**:
    - A **List** is an ordered collection that allows duplicates. Elements in a list can be accessed by their index.
    - Kotlin provides two types of lists:

- **Immutable lists**: Created using `listOf()`, and you cannot modify the contents after creation.
- **Mutable lists**: Created using `mutableListOf()`, and you can add, remove, or change elements.

Example:

```kotlin
val immutableList = listOf(1, 2, 3, 4, 5)
val mutableList = mutableListOf(1, 2, 3)
mutableList.add(4)  // Mutable lists allow
modification
```

Key Points:

- `listOf()` creates an immutable list.
- `mutableListOf()` creates a mutable list.

2. **Sets**:
   - A **Set** is an unordered collection of unique elements. No duplicates are allowed in a set.
   - Kotlin provides two types of sets:
     - **Immutable sets**: Created using `setOf()`.
     - **Mutable sets**: Created using `mutableSetOf()`.

75

Example:

```kotlin
val immutableSet = setOf(1, 2, 3, 4, 5)
val mutableSet = mutableSetOf(1, 2, 3)
mutableSet.add(4)   // Mutable sets allow modification
mutableSet.add(3)   // Duplicate value will be ignored
```

Key Points:

- **setOf()** creates an immutable set.
- **mutableSetOf()** creates a mutable set.

3. **Maps**:
   - A **Map** is a collection of key-value pairs. Each key is unique, but the values can be duplicates.
   - Kotlin provides two types of maps:
     - **Immutable maps**: Created using mapOf().
     - **Mutable maps**: Created using mutableMapOf().

Example:

```kotlin
```

```kotlin
val immutableMap = mapOf("key1" to
"value1", "key2" to "value2")
val mutableMap = mutableMapOf("key1" to
"value1")
mutableMap["key2"] = "value2"  // Mutable
maps allow modification
```

Key Points:

- o **mapOf()** creates an immutable map.
- o **mutableMapOf()** creates a mutable map.
- o Use the to keyword to create key-value pairs (e.g., "key1" to "value1").

Iterating Over Collections

Kotlin provides several ways to iterate over collections. You can use loops, such as **for** loops, or higher-order functions, such as forEach.

1. **For Loop**: A basic **for** loop allows you to iterate over a collection by referencing each element.

Example:

```kotlin
kotlin

val list = listOf(1, 2, 3, 4, 5)
```

77

```
for (item in list) {
    println(item)
}
```

2. **ForEach Function**: The `forEach()` function is a higher-order function that allows you to iterate over collections and perform actions for each element.

   Example:

   ```kotlin
   val set = setOf(1, 2, 3, 4, 5)
   set.forEach { println(it) }
   ```

3. **For Loop with Indices**: If you need to access both the index and the value, you can use the `indices` property or the `withIndex()` function.

   Example:

   ```kotlin
   val list = listOf("apple", "banana", "cherry")
   for (index in list.indices) {
       println("Element at index $index is ${list[index]}")
   }
   ```

Example using `withIndex()`:

```kotlin
list.withIndex().forEach {
    println("Element at index ${it.index}
is ${it.value}")
}
```

Filtering, Transforming, and Sorting Data

Kotlin's collection library provides many useful functions for manipulating data. These functions allow you to **filter**, **transform**, and **sort** your collections with ease.

1. **Filtering**: The `filter()` function creates a new collection by filtering out elements that don't satisfy a condition.

   Example:

   ```kotlin
   val numbers = listOf(1, 2, 3, 4, 5, 6)
   val evenNumbers = numbers.filter { it % 2
   == 0 }
   println(evenNumbers)  // Output: [2, 4, 6]
   ```

○ **filter()** returns a list of elements that satisfy the condition.

You can also use **filterNot()** to exclude elements that meet a condition.

Example:

```kotlin
val oddNumbers = numbers.filterNot { it %
2 == 0 }
println(oddNumbers)  // Output: [1, 3, 5]
```

2. **Transforming**: The **map()** function allows you to transform each element of a collection to a new form.

Example:

```kotlin
val words = listOf("apple", "banana",
"cherry")
val uppercaseWords = words.map {
it.uppercase() }
println(uppercaseWords)    // Output:
[APPLE, BANANA, CHERRY]
```

    o **map()** returns a new list with transformed elements.

3. **Sorting**: Kotlin provides sorting functions like **sorted()**, **sortedBy()**, and **sortedDescending()**.

Example:

```kotlin
kotlin


val numbers = listOf(5, 3, 8, 1, 2)
val sortedNumbers = numbers.sorted()
println(sortedNumbers)  // Output: [1, 2, 3, 5, 8]
```

You can also sort objects based on a property using **sortedBy()**.

Example:

```kotlin
kotlin


val words = listOf("apple", "banana", "cherry")
val sortedWords = words.sortedBy { it.length }
println(sortedWords)  // Output: [apple, banana, cherry]
```

4. **Reversing**: You can reverse the order of elements using **reversed()**.

Example:

```kotlin
val numbers = listOf(1, 2, 3, 4, 5)
val reversedNumbers = numbers.reversed()
println(reversedNumbers)  // Output: [5, 4, 3, 2, 1]
```

Handling Nullability with Collections

Kotlin provides robust null safety, which extends to collections as well. You can create collections that contain nullable elements or collections that themselves can be `null`.

1. **Nullable Elements in Collections**: You can have collections that contain nullable elements. The type of the collection's elements must explicitly include ? to allow null values.

Example:

```kotlin
```

```
val    nullableList:    List<String?>    =
listOf("apple", null, "banana")
println(nullableList)  // Output: [apple,
null, banana]
```

2. **Nullable Collections**: You can also have nullable collections, which means the entire collection can be null.

   Example:

   ```
   kotlin
   ```

   ```
   val nullableSet: Set<String>? = null
   println(nullableSet)  // Output: null
   ```

3. **Safe Collection Operations**: To safely handle nullable collections, you can use the **safe call operator (?.)** or the **Elvis operator (?:)**.

   Example:

   ```
   kotlin
   ```

   ```
   val    nullableList:    List<String>?    =
   listOf("apple", "banana")
   val size = nullableList?.size ?: 0
   println(size) // Output: 2 (if the list is
   null, size defaults to 0)
   ```

o The safe call operator (?.) is used to access the property or method of a nullable collection without causing a `NullPointerException`.

o The Elvis operator (?:) provides a default value when the collection is `null`.

Key Takeaways

- **Collections in Kotlin**: Kotlin provides **Lists**, **Sets**, and **Maps** for storing data, each with immutable and mutable versions.

- **Iterating**: You can iterate over collections using basic loops or higher-order functions like `forEach`.

- **Manipulating Data**: Kotlin's collection library provides powerful functions like `filter()`, `map()`, `sorted()`, and `reversed()` for filtering, transforming, and sorting data.

- **Nullability**: Kotlin's null safety extends to collections, allowing you to handle nullable elements and nullable collections with ease.

In the next chapters, we'll continue to explore more advanced techniques for working with collections and handling data in Kotlin.

CHAPTER 8

ANDROID UI: VIEWS AND LAYOUTS

In this chapter, we will explore Android's **UI components** and **layouts**. The UI (User Interface) is a critical part of every Android app, and understanding how to build and manage views and layouts is essential for creating intuitive and interactive applications. We will cover how to use basic views like **TextView**, **Button**, and **ImageView**, and then move on to layout management using **LinearLayout**, **RelativeLayout**, and **ConstraintLayout**. We will also discuss handling user input using **EditText** and **Button**.

Introduction to Android UI Components

Android provides a rich set of **UI components** (also called **views**) that are used to display and interact with content. These components form the building blocks of any Android app's interface. Each view in Android is a subclass of the `View` class, which is the fundamental building block for all UI elements.

1. **View**: The base class for UI elements. Views are typically widgets like buttons, text fields, and images.

2. **ViewGroup**: A special type of view that can contain other views. Layouts like `LinearLayout`, `RelativeLayout`, and `ConstraintLayout` are subclasses of `ViewGroup` and are used to arrange views within them.

Let's explore some basic UI components (views) that you'll frequently use in Android apps.

Using TextView, Button, ImageView, and More

1. **TextView**: The `TextView` widget is used to display text on the screen. You can customize its properties like font size, color, alignment, and more.

   Example:

```xml
<TextView
    android:id="@+id/textView"
    android:layout_width="wrap_content"
    android:layout_height="wrap_content"
    android:text="Hello, Kotlin!"
    android:textSize="18sp"
    android:textColor="#000000"

    android:layout_centerHorizontal="true"/>
```

In this example:

- o `android:text` specifies the text to be displayed.
- o `android:textSize` sets the size of the text.
- o `android:textColor` sets the color of the text.

In Kotlin (Activity):

```kotlin
val textView: TextView =
findViewById(R.id.textView)
textView.text = "Updated Text"
```

2. **Button**: The `Button` widget is used for creating clickable buttons. You can handle user interactions with buttons using event listeners like `setOnClickListener`.

Example:

```xml
<Button
    android:id="@+id/button"
    android:layout_width="wrap_content"
    android:layout_height="wrap_content"
    android:text="Click Me"/>
```

In Kotlin (Activity):

```kotlin
kotlin
```

```kotlin
val          button:          Button          =
findViewById(R.id.button)
button.setOnClickListener {
    Toast.makeText(this,          "Button
clicked!", Toast.LENGTH_SHORT).show()
}
```

In this example:

- o `setOnClickListener` is used to define the action that happens when the button is clicked (in this case, showing a Toast message).

3. **ImageView**: The `ImageView` widget is used to display images. You can set an image from resources or from an external source like the web.

Example:

```xml
xml
```

```xml
<ImageView
    android:id="@+id/imageView"
    android:layout_width="wrap_content"
    android:layout_height="wrap_content"
```

88

```
android:src="@drawable/sample_image"/>
```

In Kotlin (Activity):

```kotlin
kotlin
```

```kotlin
val       imageView:       ImageView       =
findViewById(R.id.imageView)
imageView.setImageResource(R.drawable.new
_image)
```

4. **ProgressBar**: The `ProgressBar` is a UI component used to show the progress of an ongoing operation, such as a download or file .

Example:

```xml
xml
```

```xml
<ProgressBar
    android:id="@+id/progressBar"
    android:layout_width="wrap_content"
    android:layout_height="wrap_content"
    android:visibility="gone"/>
```

In Kotlin (Activity):

```kotlin
kotlin
```

```
val       progressBar:       ProgressBar     =
findViewById(R.id.progressBar)
progressBar.visibility = View.VISIBLE   //
Show progress bar
progressBar.visibility = View.GONE  // Hide
progress bar
```

Basic Layouts: LinearLayout, RelativeLayout, ConstraintLayout

Layouts are containers that manage the positioning and sizing of views. Android provides several layout types to organize and manage the UI components.

1. **LinearLayout**: The `LinearLayout` arranges its child views either vertically or horizontally in a single row or column.

   Example:

   ```
   xml

   <LinearLayout
       android:layout_width="match_parent"
       android:layout_height="match_parent"
       android:orientation="vertical">

       <TextView
   ```

```
android:layout_width="wrap_content"

android:layout_height="wrap_content"
        android:text="Hello"/>
    <Button

android:layout_width="wrap_content"

android:layout_height="wrap_content"
        android:text="Click Me"/>
</LinearLayout>
```

- o **android:orientation**: This attribute determines whether the children will be laid out horizontally or vertically.

2. **RelativeLayout**: The RelativeLayout allows you to position views relative to each other. Views can be aligned to the left, right, top, or bottom of other views or parent containers.

Example:

```
xml

<RelativeLayout
    android:layout_width="match_parent"
    android:layout_height="match_parent">
```

```xml
<TextView
    android:id="@+id/textView"

android:layout_width="wrap_content"

android:layout_height="wrap_content"
    android:text="Hello"

android:layout_centerHorizontal="true"

android:layout_alignParentTop="true"/>

    <Button
        android:id="@+id/button"

android:layout_width="wrap_content"

android:layout_height="wrap_content"
        android:text="Click Me"

android:layout_below="@id/textView"

android:layout_centerHorizontal="true"/>
</RelativeLayout>
```

- o **android:layout_alignParentTop**:
  Positions the TextView at the top of the RelativeLayout.

o **android:layout_below**:   Positions   the `Button` below the `TextView`.

3. **ConstraintLayout**: The `ConstraintLayout` is a more flexible and powerful layout that allows you to define constraints between views. It is often used for complex layouts due to its versatility.

Example:

xml

```
<androidx.constraintlayout.widget.Constra
intLayout
    android:layout_width="match_parent"
    android:layout_height="match_parent">

    <TextView
        android:id="@+id/textView"

android:layout_width="wrap_content"

android:layout_height="wrap_content"
        android:text="Hello"

app:layout_constraintTop_toTopOf="parent"

app:layout_constraintStart_toStartOf="par
ent"/>
```

```
<Button
    android:id="@+id/button"

android:layout_width="wrap_content"

android:layout_height="wrap_content"
    android:text="Click Me"

app:layout_constraintTop_toBottomOf="@id/
textView"

app:layout_constraintStart_toStartOf="par
ent"/>
</androidx.constraintlayout.widget.Constr
aintLayout>
```

- o **app:layout_constraintTop_toTopOf="p arent"**: Positions the `TextView` at the top of the `ConstraintLayout`.
- o **app:layout_constraintStart_toStartO f="parent"**: Aligns the `TextView` to the start (left side) of the layout.

Handling User Input with EditText and Button

1. **EditText**: The `EditText` view is used to receive text input from the user. You can configure it for various input types like passwords, numbers, email, etc.

Example:

xml

```
<EditText
    android:id="@+id/editText"
    android:layout_width="match_parent"
    android:layout_height="wrap_content"
    android:hint="Enter text here"
    android:inputType="text" />
```

- o **android:hint** provides a placeholder text when the field is empty.
- o **android:inputType** specifies the type of input (e.g., text, number, password).

In Kotlin (Activity):

kotlin

```
val     editText:     EditText     =
findViewById(R.id.editText)
val inputText = editText.text.toString()
```

- o editText.text.toString() retrieves the text entered by the user.

2. **Button**: You can use a Button to trigger actions when the user interacts with the UI.

Example:

xml

```
<Button
    android:id="@+id/button"
    android:layout_width="wrap_content"
    android:layout_height="wrap_content"
    android:text="Submit" />
```

In Kotlin (Activity):

kotlin

```
val       button:       Button       =
findViewById(R.id.button)
button.setOnClickListener {
    val            inputText            =
editText.text.toString()
    Toast.makeText(this,   "You   entered:
$inputText", Toast.LENGTH_SHORT).show()
}
```

  o The setOnClickListener is used to listen for
     clicks on the button and perform the
     corresponding action.

Key Takeaways

- **Views**: Basic Android UI components like `TextView`, `Button`, `ImageView`, and `EditText` are used to display text, receive input, and show images or interactive elements.

- **Layouts**: `LinearLayout`, `RelativeLayout`, and `ConstraintLayout` are used to manage the arrangement of views in an app's UI. Each layout has its specific use case based on how you want to organize elements.

- **User Input**: The `EditText` widget is used to receive input from the user, and the `Button` widget is used to trigger actions like submitting data.

In the following chapters, we will explore how to work with more advanced UI components, handle user interactions, and manage app navigation.

CHAPTER 9

FUNCTIONS AND LAMBDAS IN ANDROID DEVELOPMENT

In this chapter, we'll dive into using **functions** and **lambdas** in Android development. Lambdas are a powerful feature in Kotlin that allow you to write concise, functional code. In Android development, lambdas are often used to simplify event handling (such as button clicks) and to create more readable and efficient code. We'll explore how to pass lambdas to Android views, simplify listeners with lambdas, and incorporate functional programming approaches in Android development.

Passing Lambdas to Android Views

In Kotlin, **lambdas** are often used to handle events in Android views like buttons, text fields, and other UI components. A lambda is essentially an anonymous function that can be passed as an argument to a function or a method. Passing lambdas to views allows you to write more concise code for handling UI events.

1. **Basic Button Click with Lambda**: In Android, the most common event handler is `setOnClickListener`.

Typically, this is used to listen for button clicks and execute some logic when the button is pressed.

Without Lambda (Traditional Approach):

```kotlin
val button: Button = findViewById(R.id.button)
button.setOnClickListener(object : View.OnClickListener {
    override fun onClick(v: View?) {
        Toast.makeText(this@MainActivity,
"Button clicked",
Toast.LENGTH_SHORT).show()
    }
})
```

With Lambda (Simplified): Kotlin allows you to simplify this by using **lambda expressions**. Instead of creating an anonymous class to handle the click, you can pass the lambda directly to setOnClickListener.

```kotlin
val button: Button = findViewById(R.id.button)
button.setOnClickListener {
```

```
Toast.makeText(this, "Button clicked",
Toast.LENGTH_SHORT).show()
}
```

- o The lambda expression { ... } is passed directly to `setOnClickListener` as a function argument.
- o This approach reduces the verbosity of the code and makes it easier to read.

2. **Passing Lambdas to Other Views**: You can use lambdas to handle events for various other views, such as `TextView`, `ImageView`, and custom views.

Example for an `EditText`:

kotlin

```
val        editText:        EditText       =
findViewById(R.id.editText)
editText.addTextChangedListener { text ->
    println("Text changed: $text")
}
```

Here, the lambda expression is passed to `addTextChangedListener` to handle changes in the text entered by the user.

Simplifying Listeners Using Lambdas

Android development typically involves setting up listeners to respond to user interactions like clicks, touches, or changes. With Kotlin, lambdas simplify this process by eliminating the need for boilerplate code. Let's look at how lambdas simplify the process of setting up various listeners.

1. **OnClickListener**: Using lambdas, the `OnClickListener` becomes much more concise, as demonstrated earlier. The same principle applies to other listener types.

   Example:

   ```kotlin
   val button: Button = findViewById(R.id.button)
   button.setOnClickListener {
       // Handle click
       println("Button was clicked")
   }
   ```

2. **OnTouchListener**: Similarly, for touch events, you can use lambdas to simplify the implementation of `OnTouchListener`.

   Example:

```kotlin
val imageView: ImageView =
findViewById(R.id.imageView)
imageView.setOnTouchListener { _, event ->
    if (event.action ==
MotionEvent.ACTION_DOWN) {
        println("Image touched!")
    }
    true
}
```

- o The `setOnTouchListener` method accepts a lambda that provides the event and the view.
- o The lambda can check for specific touch actions and perform logic based on the user's interaction.

3. **OnFocusChangeListener**: You can use lambdas for focus change listeners as well.

Example:

```kotlin
val editText: EditText =
findViewById(R.id.editText)
editText.setOnFocusChangeListener { _,
hasFocus ->
    if (hasFocus) {
        println("EditText gained focus")
```

```
    } else {
        println("EditText lost focus")
    }
}
```

In this case, the lambda is used to handle the focus change of the EditText view, making the code much shorter and more readable.

Functional Programming Approaches to Android Development

Functional programming (FP) is a paradigm where functions are treated as first-class citizens. In Kotlin, you can easily adopt functional programming practices to write cleaner, more declarative code. Kotlin's support for higher-order functions, lambdas, and immutability makes it a great fit for integrating FP principles in Android development.

1. **Higher-Order Functions**: A **higher-order function** is a function that takes another function as a parameter or returns a function. In Android development, higher-order functions can be used to simplify repetitive code and enhance modularity.

    Example: A function that processes a list and applies a function to each element.

```kotlin
fun <T> List<T>.processEach(action: (T) ->
Unit) {
    for (item in this) {
        action(item)
    }
}
```

- o The `processEach` function takes an action as a parameter and applies it to each element of the list.
- o You can use this function like this:

```kotlin
val numbers = listOf(1, 2, 3, 4)
numbers.processEach { println(it) }
```

- o This is a simple example of a higher-order function that processes each element in a list using a lambda expression.

2. **Immutability**: In functional programming, **immutability** is a key concept. You avoid changing data once it's created, which makes your code easier to reason about and avoids side effects. Kotlin makes it easy to work with immutable data by using `val` (immutable variables) and

104

providing immutable collections like List, Set, and Map.

Example:

```kotlin
val numbers = listOf(1, 2, 3, 4)
val updatedNumbers = numbers.map { it * 2 }
println(updatedNumbers)  // Output: [2, 4, 6, 8]
```

- o In this example, numbers is immutable, and we create a new list updatedNumbers by applying a transformation using map. The original list is not modified.

3. **Using let, apply, also, and run**: Kotlin provides several scope functions such as let, apply, also, and run, which make working with objects and lambdas more elegant. These functions can help streamline your code by reducing the need for explicit null checks and making your code more concise.

- o **let**: Executes a block of code on an object and returns the result.

```kotlin
```

```
val name: String? = "Kotlin"
name?.let { println("Name is: $it")
}
```

- ○ **apply**: Used to initialize an object and return the object itself.

kotlin

```
val button = Button(this).apply {
    text = "Click Me"
    setOnClickListener                {
println("Button clicked") }
}
```

- ○ **also**: Similar to let, but returns the object itself instead of the result of the lambda.

kotlin

```
val button = Button(this).also {
println("Button created: $it") }
```

- ○ **run**: Executes a block of code and returns the result of the block.

kotlin

```
val greeting = "Hello".run {
    this + ", Kotlin!"
```

106

```
}
println(greeting)   // Output: Hello,
Kotlin!
```

4. **Using Collections with Functional Operations**: Kotlin's standard library provides a rich set of functional operations that allow you to process collections efficiently and declaratively. Operations like `filter()`, `map()`, `reduce()`, and `fold()` can help you manipulate and transform data in a functional way.

Example:

```kotlin
val numbers = listOf(1, 2, 3, 4, 5)
val doubled = numbers.map { it * 2 }
val sum = numbers.filter { it % 2 == 0
}.sum()
```

- o `map` is used to transform each element of the collection.
- o `filter` is used to extract elements that meet a certain condition.
- o `sum` is used to compute the sum of elements in the filtered collection.

Key Takeaways

- **Lambdas in Android**: Lambdas make event handling (such as button clicks) and view interactions more concise and easier to manage.
- **Simplified Listeners**: You can simplify Android listeners (like `OnClickListener`, `OnTouchListener`, etc.) using lambdas, reducing boilerplate code.
- **Functional Programming**: Kotlin supports functional programming techniques like higher-order functions, immutability, and lambda expressions. These approaches can lead to more readable, modular, and efficient Android code.

In the next chapters, we will explore more advanced functional programming concepts in Kotlin and how to apply them in Android development to build better, more maintainable applications.

CHAPTER 10

KOTLIN COROUTINES AND CONCURRENCY

In this chapter, we will explore **Kotlin coroutines** and their role in handling **concurrency** in Android development. Concurrency refers to performing multiple tasks at the same time, which is crucial for responsive applications. In Android, if you perform long-running tasks (like network requests or database operations) on the main thread, it can cause the app to freeze or become unresponsive, leading to **ANR (Application Not Responding)** errors. Kotlin coroutines help solve this issue by providing a way to manage background tasks efficiently and without blocking the main thread.

What Are Coroutines?

A **coroutine** is a lightweight thread-like structure that enables asynchronous programming in Kotlin. Unlike traditional threads, coroutines are more efficient because they are non-blocking and can be suspended and resumed without consuming system resources.

Key features of Kotlin coroutines:

- **Lightweight**: Coroutines are much lighter than threads. You can run thousands of coroutines concurrently without significant overhead.

- **Non-blocking**: Coroutines allow you to write asynchronous code in a sequential manner, improving readability and maintainability.

- **Suspending functions**: Coroutines allow functions to be "suspended" and resumed without blocking threads. This makes them ideal for tasks like network calls, file I/O, or long computations.

- **Structured concurrency**: Kotlin provides mechanisms to manage the lifecycle and cancellation of coroutines, making it easier to handle complex concurrency scenarios.

Kotlin coroutines are based on the idea of **suspending functions** and **dispatchers**. Coroutines can be suspended and resumed at a later point without blocking the current thread.

Basic Coroutine Setup and Usage

To start using Kotlin coroutines, you'll need to add the necessary dependencies to your project. These dependencies are provided by the Kotlin Coroutines library.

1. **Adding Dependencies**: In your `build.gradle` file (app module), add the following dependencies:

```gradle
dependencies {
    implementation
"org.jetbrains.kotlinx:kotlinx-
coroutines-android:1.5.2"
    implementation
"org.jetbrains.kotlinx:kotlinx-
coroutines-core:1.5.2"
}
```

2. **Creating a Coroutine**: You can start a coroutine using the `launch` or `async` function. These functions are used to define coroutines and run them in different **dispatchers** (threads or thread pools).

Example (Using `launch` to start a Coroutine):

```kotlin
import kotlinx.coroutines.*

// Launching a coroutine
GlobalScope.launch(Dispatchers.Main) {
    // Code to run on the main thread
    delay(1000)  // Non-blocking delay
```

```
    println("Coroutine completed")
}
```

In this example:

- o GlobalScope.launch(Dispatchers.Main) creates a coroutine that runs on the **main thread** (UI thread).
- o delay(1000) is a suspending function that delays the coroutine for 1000 milliseconds without blocking the thread.

Example (Using async to start a Coroutine):

```kotlin
GlobalScope.async(Dispatchers.IO) {
    // Run background task (e.g., network
request or database query)
    val result = fetchDataFromNetwork()
    return@async result
}
```

In this case:

- o async is used to launch a coroutine that runs asynchronously and returns a result.
- o Dispatchers.IO is used for I/O-bound tasks like network requests.

3. **Launching Coroutines in the Main Activity**: In a typical Android app, you will use **lifecycleScope** or **viewModelScope** for managing coroutines in activities and view models, as these scopes automatically cancel coroutines when the associated lifecycle is destroyed.

Example:

kotlin

```
lifecycleScope.launch {
    val data = fetchDataFromNetwork() //
Simulate a network call
    updateUIWithData(data)    // Update UI
with the fetched data
}
```

o lifecycleScope.launch ensures that the coroutine is canceled when the activity or fragment is destroyed, preventing memory leaks.

Async Tasks and Threading in Android

In Android, long-running tasks like network calls, database queries, or file I/O should always be done on background threads to avoid blocking the main (UI) thread. Blocking the main thread can lead to **ANR** (Application Not Responding) errors. Kotlin coroutines make it easy to offload tasks to background threads.

1. **Asynchronous Tasks with `async` and `await`**: The **async** coroutine builder is used to perform asynchronous operations and return results. You can use **await()** to get the result of an `async` operation when it's ready.

   Example:

   ```kotlin
   val deferred: Deferred<String> = GlobalScope.async {
       // Simulating a long-running task, e.g., a network call
       delay(2000) // Non-blocking delay
       "Hello from the background!"
   }

   // Await the result on the main thread
   val result = deferred.await()
   println(result) // Output: Hello from the background!
   ```

   o **Deferred** is a non-blocking representation of a future value.

o **await()** is used to get the result of the `async` coroutine, and it suspends the current coroutine until the result is available.

2. **Threading with `Dispatchers`**: Kotlin coroutines allow you to specify the **dispatcher** on which the coroutine will run. There are several types of dispatchers:

   o **`Dispatchers.Main`**: For running tasks on the main thread (UI thread).

   o **`Dispatchers.IO`**: For I/O-bound tasks, like network or disk operations.

   o **`Dispatchers.Default`**: For CPU-intensive tasks, like complex calculations.

   o **`Dispatchers.Unconfined`**: A dispatcher that doesn't confine the coroutine to any particular thread.

Example (Performing I/O on a background thread):

```kotlin
GlobalScope.launch(Dispatchers.IO) {
    val data = fetchDataFromNetwork()   //
Simulate network call
    withContext(Dispatchers.Main) {
        // Switch back to the main thread
to update the UI
        updateUIWithData(data)
    }
```

```
}
```

- ○ **withContext(Dispatchers.Main)** is used to switch from the background thread back to the main thread for UI updates.

Avoiding ANR (Application Not Responding) Errors

In Android, the **ANR (Application Not Responding)** error occurs when the main (UI) thread is blocked for more than 5 seconds. This usually happens when long-running tasks (such as network requests or database operations) are executed on the main thread. To avoid ANR errors, you should always perform these tasks on a background thread.

1. **Performing Long-Running Tasks Off the Main Thread**: Coroutines allow you to easily switch long-running tasks to background threads, keeping the UI responsive.

   Example:

   ```kotlin
   lifecycleScope.launch {
       // Perform the long-running task on a
   background thread
   ```

```
val                result              =
withContext(Dispatchers.IO) {
        fetchDataFromNetwork()              //
Simulate a network call
    }
    // Update the UI on the main thread
    updateUIWithData(result)
}
```

- o **withContext(Dispatchers.IO)** switches the coroutine to a background thread for I/O-bound tasks.
- o The result of the network call is then returned to the main thread for UI updates.

2. **Avoiding Long Tasks on the Main Thread**: Common tasks that should never be performed on the main thread include:
   - o Network requests
   - o File I/O operations
   - o Heavy calculations

Always use **Dispatchers.IO** for network or disk operations and **Dispatchers.Default** for CPU-intensive work to ensure the main thread remains unblocked.

Key Takeaways

- **Coroutines**: Kotlin coroutines are lightweight and non-blocking threads that make it easier to perform asynchronous tasks without blocking the main thread. They are essential for creating responsive Android apps.

- **Async Tasks and Threading**: Use `async` for asynchronous tasks and `await()` to get results from background tasks. Coroutines provide an easy way to offload tasks from the main thread to background threads using different dispatchers.

- **Avoiding ANR**: To avoid ANR (Application Not Responding) errors, ensure that long-running tasks (network calls, database operations, etc.) are performed on background threads (e.g., using `Dispatchers.IO`), keeping the main thread free for UI updates.

In the next chapters, we will continue to explore more advanced uses of Kotlin coroutines and how they can be used to manage complex concurrency patterns in Android development.

CHAPTER 11

DATA PERSISTENCE: SHAREDPREFERENCES AND SQLITE

In this chapter, we will explore **data persistence** in Android development, focusing on how to store and retrieve data in Android apps. We will cover two common methods for data storage: **SharedPreferences** and **SQLite**. We will also discuss **Room**, which provides an abstraction layer over SQLite, making database interactions easier and more manageable in Android development.

Introduction to SharedPreferences

SharedPreferences is a simple key-value storage system that allows you to store small pieces of data, such as user preferences or settings. This data is stored in a private file and persists across app restarts. It's commonly used for storing simple data like login credentials, preferences, or app settings.

1. **When to Use SharedPreferences**:

- Storing simple data (e.g., booleans, strings, integers).
- Storing small datasets that don't require complex queries or relationships.
- Ideal for saving user settings, theme preferences, etc.

2. **Saving Data Using SharedPreferences**: To write data to SharedPreferences, you need to get an instance of SharedPreferences and use the Editor object to modify the data.

Example:

kotlin

```
val             sharedPreferences            =
getSharedPreferences("MyPreferences",
Context.MODE_PRIVATE)
val editor = sharedPreferences.edit()
editor.putString("username", "john_doe")
editor.putInt("user_age", 25)
editor.apply()          //    Apply    changes
asynchronously
```

- **getSharedPreferences()** retrieves the SharedPreferences instance.
- **putString()** and **putInt()** are used to save key-value pairs.

o **apply()** commits the changes asynchronously.

3. **Retrieving Data from SharedPreferences**: You can retrieve data from `SharedPreferences` using the appropriate `get` methods.

Example:

```kotlin
```

```kotlin
val             sharedPreferences          =
getSharedPreferences("MyPreferences",
Context.MODE_PRIVATE)
val             username                   =
sharedPreferences.getString("username",
"default_value")  // "default_value" is the
fallback
val             userAge                    =
sharedPreferences.getInt("user_age",     0)
// Default value is 0
```

o **getString()** and **getInt()** are used to fetch the data. If the key doesn't exist, the default value is returned.

4. **Clearing SharedPreferences**: You can clear all the data in `SharedPreferences` using the `clear()` method.

Example:

```kotlin
```

```
val editor = sharedPreferences.edit()
editor.clear()      // Remove all saved
preferences
editor.apply()
```

Working with SQLite Databases

SQLite is a relational database engine that stores data in a local file. Android provides built-in support for SQLite, allowing you to perform SQL operations like querying, inserting, updating, and deleting data. SQLite is suitable for storing structured data that requires complex querying and relationships between entities.

1. **When to Use SQLite**:
    - Storing complex data or large datasets.
    - When you need to perform complex queries, such as sorting or filtering data.
    - Managing relationships between entities (e.g., one-to-many, many-to-many).
2. **Setting Up SQLite in Android**: To work with SQLite, you need to create a SQLiteOpenHelper class, which helps manage database creation and version management.

Example:

```
kotlin
```

```kotlin
class MyDatabaseHelper(context: Context) :
SQLiteOpenHelper(context, DATABASE_NAME,
null, DATABASE_VERSION) {

    override fun onCreate(db:
SQLiteDatabase?) {
        val createTableQuery = "CREATE
TABLE $TABLE_NAME (id INTEGER PRIMARY KEY,
name TEXT, age INTEGER)"
        db?.execSQL(createTableQuery)
    }

    override fun onUpgrade(db:
SQLiteDatabase?, oldVersion: Int,
newVersion: Int) {
        db?.execSQL("DROP TABLE IF EXISTS
$TABLE_NAME")
        onCreate(db)
    }

    companion object {
        private const val DATABASE_NAME =
"my_database"
        private const val DATABASE_VERSION
= 1
        private const val TABLE_NAME =
"users"
    }
}
```

123

- o **onCreate()** is called when the database is created for the first time.
- o **onUpgrade()** handles database schema changes (e.g., adding new tables or columns).

3. **Inserting Data into SQLite**: To insert data into the database, you use the `insert()` method on the `SQLiteDatabase` object.

Example:

```kotlin
val                db                =
MyDatabaseHelper(context).writableDatabas
e
val values = ContentValues().apply {
    put("name", "John Doe")
    put("age", 30)
}
db.insert("users", null, values)
```

- o **ContentValues** is used to store the data that will be inserted into the table.

4. **Querying Data from SQLite**: To retrieve data from the database, you use the `query()` method on the `SQLiteDatabase` object.

Example:

```kotlin
val db =
MyDatabaseHelper(context).readableDatabas
e
val cursor = db.query("users",
arrayOf("id", "name", "age"), null, null,
null, null, null)
if (cursor.moveToFirst()) {
    val name =
cursor.getString(cursor.getColumnIndex("n
ame"))
    val age =
cursor.getInt(cursor.getColumnIndex("age"
))
    println("Name: $name, Age: $age")
}
cursor.close()
```

- o **cursor** is used to iterate through the rows of data returned by the query.

Storing and Retrieving Data with Kotlin

Kotlin provides a more concise way to handle data storage and retrieval in SQLite by using extension functions and working with objects directly.

125

1. **Creating a Data Model**: It's a good practice to create a data model class to represent each row in the database.

   Example:

   ```kotlin
   data class User(val id: Int, val name: String, val age: Int)
   ```

2. **Storing Data Using SQLite**: Instead of manually adding each value to `ContentValues`, you can create an extension function to simplify this process.

   Example:

   ```kotlin
   fun SQLiteDatabase.insertUser(user: User) {
       val values = ContentValues().apply {
           put("name", user.name)
           put("age", user.age)
       }
       insert("users", null, values)
   }
   ```

3. **Retrieving Data Using SQLite**: You can create an extension function to convert rows of data into model objects.

Example:

```
kotlin


fun Cursor.toUser(): User {
    val id = getInt(getColumnIndex("id"))
    val                name                 =
getString(getColumnIndex("name"))
    val                age                  =
getInt(getColumnIndex("age"))
    return User(id, name, age)
}


val    cursor    =    db.query("users",
arrayOf("id", "name", "age"), null, null,
null, null, null)
if (cursor.moveToFirst()) {
    val user = cursor.toUser()
    println("User: $user")
}
cursor.close()
```

Using Room Database for Android Development

Room is an abstraction layer over SQLite that simplifies database interactions in Android. Room handles the boilerplate code required to manage SQLite, such as creating tables, handling schema migrations, and performing queries. It uses **annotations** to define entities, DAOs (Data Access Objects), and databases.

1. **Setting Up Room**: To use Room, you need to add the necessary dependencies in your `build.gradle` file.

   `gradle`

   ```
   dependencies {
       implementation    "androidx.room:room-
   runtime:2.3.0"
       kapt              "androidx.room:room-
   compiler:2.3.0"
   }
   ```

   Note: Don't forget to enable **KAPT** for annotation processing in your project.

2. **Defining an Entity**: An **entity** represents a table in the database. You define entities using the `@Entity` annotation.

   Example:

```kotlin
@Entity(tableName = "users")
data class User(
    @PrimaryKey(autoGenerate = true) val
id: Int,
    val name: String,
    val age: Int
)
```

- o The @PrimaryKey annotation marks the primary key column, and autoGenerate = true means the ID will be automatically generated.

3. **Creating a DAO (Data Access Object)**: A **DAO** is an interface that defines the database operations (queries, insertions, etc.) for an entity.

Example:

```kotlin
@Dao
interface UserDao {
    @Insert
    suspend fun insertUser(user: User)

    @Query("SELECT * FROM users")
    suspend fun getAllUsers(): List<User>
}
```

o The `@Insert` annotation defines an insert operation, and `@Query` allows you to define custom SQL queries.

4. **Creating a Room Database**: The `@Database` annotation defines the database, including the entities and the DAO.

Example:

```kotlin
@Database(entities = [User::class], version = 1)
abstract class AppDatabase : RoomDatabase() {
    abstract fun userDao(): UserDao
}
```

5. **Accessing the Database**: You can get an instance of the Room database and access the DAO to perform operations.

Example:

```kotlin
val db = Room.databaseBuilder(applicationContext,
AppDatabase::class.java,
"app_database").build()
```

```kotlin
val userDao = db.userDao()

// Insert a user
val user = User(id = 0, name = "Alice", age
= 30)
userDao.insertUser(user)

// Retrieve all users
val users = userDao.getAllUsers()
```

Key Takeaways

- **SharedPreferences**: Best suited for storing simple key-value data like settings or preferences.
- **SQLite**: Used for storing structured data and supporting complex queries and relationships.
- **Room**: A modern, simplified way to work with SQLite in Android, providing a clean abstraction with annotations and a DAO layer.
- **Data Storage with Kotlin**: Kotlin's concise syntax and extensions make working with databases easier, with less boilerplate code for storing and retrieving data.

In the next chapters, we will continue to explore advanced techniques for data persistence and how to manage large-scale data in Android applications.

CHAPTER 12

MANAGING APP RESOURCES

In this chapter, we'll dive into the important topic of **app resources** in Android development. Managing resources like images, strings, styles, dimensions, and colors is key to building flexible and scalable applications. We will also discuss how to handle **internationalization (i18n)** and **localization (l10n)** to support multiple languages and regions.

Understanding Drawables, Strings, and Styles

1. **Drawables**:

    o **Drawables** are graphical resources that can be used for backgrounds, images, icons, or shapes in your app. They can be defined as XML files, image files, or shape files.

    o Drawables are stored in the `res/drawable` directory.

Types of Drawables:

    o **Bitmap Drawables**: Image files such as PNG, JPEG, or GIF.

- o **Vector Drawables**: Scalable XML-based images, often used for icons. They are especially useful for supporting multiple screen densities.
- o **Shape Drawables**: Defined with XML to create simple geometric shapes like rectangles, circles, and lines.

Example (Bitmap Drawable):

```xml
<ImageView
    android:layout_width="wrap_content"
    android:layout_height="wrap_content"
    android:src="@drawable/sample_image"
/>
```

Example (Vector Drawable):

```xml
<ImageView
    android:layout_width="wrap_content"
    android:layout_height="wrap_content"

android:src="@drawable/ic_sample_icon" />
```

2. **Strings**:

- o **Strings** are used for storing textual data such as labels, messages, and user interface content. They are stored in the `res/values/strings.xml` file.
- o **String resources** are ideal for supporting internationalization, as they can be easily replaced with localized versions.

Example (strings.xml):

```xml
<resources>
    <string name="app_name">My Application</string>
    <string name="welcome_message">Welcome to the app!</string>
</resources>
```

You can refer to these strings in your layout or Kotlin code:

In XML (TextView):

```xml
<TextView

android:text="@string/welcome_message" />
```

134

In Kotlin:

```kotlin
kotlin

val          welcomeMessage          =
getString(R.string.welcome_message)
```

3. **Styles**:

   o **Styles** allow you to define a collection of attributes that can be applied to multiple views to ensure a consistent look and feel.

   o Styles   are   defined   in   the `res/values/styles.xml` file.

Example (styles.xml):

```xml
xml

<resources>
    <style          name="AppTheme"
parent="Theme.AppCompat.Light.DarkActionB
ar">
        <item
name="android:textColor">@color/colorPrim
ary</item>
        <item
name="android:textSize">16sp</item>
    </style>
</resources>
```

135

You can apply styles to views like this:

In XML:

```
xml
```

```
<TextView
    style="@style/AppTheme"
    android:text="Hello World" />
```

Styles can be particularly useful when applying consistent fonts, colors, margins, or padding throughout the app.

Working with Dimensions, Colors, and Themes

1. **Dimensions**:
   - **Dimensions** define the size of UI components (e.g., width, height, padding) and are stored in the `res/values/dimens.xml` file.
   - Dimensions are useful for managing different screen sizes and densities.

Example (dimens.xml):

```
xml
```

```
<resources>
```

```
    <dimen
name="padding_small">8dp</dimen>
    <dimen
name="padding_large">16dp</dimen>
</resources>
```

You can reference these dimensions in your XML layouts:

```
xml

<TextView

android:layout_marginStart="@dimen/paddin
g_small"

android:layout_marginEnd="@dimen/padding_
large" />
```

2. **Colors**:

   o **Colors** define the color palette of your app and are stored in the `res/values/colors.xml` file.

   o Colors are useful for creating a cohesive and visually appealing design, especially when used in combination with themes.

   Example (colors.xml):

```xml
```

```xml
<resources>
    <color
name="colorPrimary">#FF5733</color>
    <color
name="colorAccent">#4CAF50</color>
</resources>
```

You can reference these colors in your XML layouts or in your code:

In XML:

```xml
```

```xml
<TextView

android:textColor="@color/colorPrimary" />
```

In Kotlin:

```kotlin
```

```kotlin
val            primaryColor            =
ContextCompat.getColor(context,
R.color.colorPrimary)
```

3. **Themes**:

- o **Themes** are collections of style attributes that are applied globally to your app or a specific activity. They are defined in the `res/values/styles.xml` file.

- o Themes define the overall look and feel of your app, such as colors, text sizes, and the appearance of system UI elements.

Example (styles.xml):

xml

```
<style                  name="AppTheme"
parent="Theme.MaterialComponents.DayNight
.DarkActionBar">
    <item
name="colorPrimary">@color/colorPrimary</
item>
    <item
name="colorAccent">@color/colorAccent</it
em>
</style>
```

You can apply the theme to your app in the `AndroidManifest.xml` file:

xml

```
<application
```

```
android:theme="@style/AppTheme">
```

Internationalization and Localization in Android Apps

Internationalization (i18n) and **Localization (l10n)** are processes that make your app adaptable to different languages, regions, and cultures. **i18n** refers to designing your app so it can easily be adapted to various languages, while **l10n** refers to the actual adaptation of the app to specific languages or regions.

1. **Internationalization (i18n)**: Internationalization involves designing your app so that it can support multiple languages and regions. This is typically achieved by using resource files (e.g., `strings.xml`, `colors.xml`) that can be easily swapped out based on the user's locale.

    o **Use Resource Files**: Store all text in `strings.xml` and all drawable images, icons, and colors in their respective resource directories.

    o **Use Format Strings**: Avoid hardcoding text in your code. Use format strings for dynamic content.

2. **Localization (l10n)**: Localization involves translating the app's content into different languages and adjusting the layout to suit local conventions (e.g., right-to-left text for languages like Arabic).

Steps for Localization:

140

- o Create `strings.xml` files for each supported language in the `res/values-<languageCode>` folder (e.g., `res/values-es` for Spanish).
- o Translate the text in the `strings.xml` file for each language.

Example (English `strings.xml`):

xml

```
<resources>
    <string name="welcome_message">Welcome to the app!</string>
</resources>
```

Example (Spanish `strings.xml`):

xml

```
<resources>
    <string name="welcome_message">¡Bienvenido a la aplicación!</string>
</resources>
```

Android will automatically load the appropriate `strings.xml` file based on the user's language preferences.

141

3. **Supporting Right-to-Left Languages**: If your app needs to support **right-to-left (RTL)** languages (like Arabic or Hebrew), Android automatically handles text direction for you. However, you need to ensure that your layouts support RTL by using the appropriate layout attributes.

Example:

```xml
xml

<TextView

android:text="@string/welcome_message"
    android:textDirection="anyRtl" />
```

This ensures that the text will be displayed correctly in both left-to-right and right-to-left languages.

4. **Handling Different Screen Sizes and Densities**: Android supports various screen sizes, densities, and aspect ratios. You can provide different resources (such as images and layout files) for different screen configurations.

   o Use `res/drawable-mdpi/`, `res/drawable-hdpi/`, and so on to provide images for different screen densities.

   o Use `res/layout-large/` or `res/layout-xlarge/` for larger screen sizes (e.g., tablets).

142

Android will automatically choose the appropriate resources based on the device's screen size and density.

Key Takeaways

- **Drawables**: Graphics like images, icons, and shapes are stored in the `drawable` folder. Vector drawables are particularly useful for icons as they scale across different screen densities.

- **Strings and Styles**: Store text and UI elements in `strings.xml` and styles in `styles.xml` to promote reusability and internationalization.

- **Dimensions and Colors**: Define consistent dimensions (e.g., padding, margins) and colors in `dimens.xml` and `colors.xml` to maintain a cohesive look across different devices.

- **Themes**: Apply global styles and themes to manage the overall look and feel of your app.

- **Internationalization and Localization**: Design your app to support multiple languages and regions by storing text in `strings.xml` and creating language-specific resource files for each locale.

In the next chapters, we will continue to explore advanced resource management techniques and how to optimize the user experience across different devices and locales.

CHAPTER 13

HANDLING USER INPUT AND FORMS

In this chapter, we'll explore how to handle user input in Android applications. User input is a crucial part of most Android apps, whether it's text entered by the user, selections made with checkboxes or radio buttons, or toggles using switches. We'll cover form validation, user feedback, event handling (such as onClickListeners), and how to use UI components like **Checkboxes**, **RadioButtons**, and **Switches** effectively.

Form Validation and User Feedback

Form validation ensures that the data entered by the user is correct and follows the expected format. It's a vital part of the user experience, as it prevents users from submitting invalid or incomplete data. In Android, you can use EditText views for text input and validate this input before allowing the user to proceed.

1. **Validating Text Input**: You can validate user input in EditText fields using Kotlin. For example, you may

145

want to ensure that the user has entered a valid email address or that a password meets specific criteria.

Example:

kotlin

```
val      editTextEmail:      EditText     =
findViewById(R.id.editTextEmail)
val email = editTextEmail.text.toString()

val emailPattern = "[a-zA-Z0-9._-]+@[a-zA-
Z0-9.-]+\\.[a-zA-Z]{2,4}"
if (email.matches(emailPattern.toRegex()))
{
    Toast.makeText(this, "Email is valid",
Toast.LENGTH_SHORT).show()
} else {
    Toast.makeText(this,  "Please  enter  a
valid email", Toast.LENGTH_SHORT).show()
}
```

- o The matches() function is used to validate the email address against a regular expression.
- o If the input matches the pattern, a success message is shown; otherwise, the user is prompted to enter a valid email.

146

2. **Using `TextWatcher` for Real-Time Validation**: You can use `TextWatcher` to validate input in real-time, providing immediate feedback to the user.

Example:

```kotlin
val editTextPassword: EditText = findViewById(R.id.editTextPassword)
editTextPassword.addTextChangedListener(object : TextWatcher {
    override fun beforeTextChanged(s: CharSequence?, start: Int, count: Int, after: Int) {}
    override fun onTextChanged(s: CharSequence?, start: Int, before: Int, count: Int) {}
    override fun afterTextChanged(s: Editable?) {
        if (s != null && s.length < 6) {
            editTextPassword.error = "Password too short"
        }
    }
})
```

147

o In this example, the password field is checked after each change, and an error message is displayed if the password is too short.

3. **Feedback for Valid/Invalid Input**:

o Use **Toast** to provide feedback to users when they submit the form with valid or invalid data.

o For more prominent feedback, you can use **Snackbar** for showing messages at the bottom of the screen or **AlertDialog** for more complex feedback.

Implementing onClickListeners *and Other Event Handlers*

In Android, **onClickListener** is one of the most commonly used event handlers, and it's essential for handling user interactions with buttons and other clickable views. However, Android provides several other event handlers for different types of user input.

1. **Setting up onClickListener for Buttons**: You can use the setOnClickListener method to define the action that should occur when a button is clicked.

Example:

```kotlin
```

```kotlin
val      buttonSubmit:      Button      =
findViewById(R.id.buttonSubmit)
buttonSubmit.setOnClickListener {
    val              username              =
editTextUsername.text.toString()
    val              password              =
editTextPassword.text.toString()

    if      (username.isEmpty()          ||
password.isEmpty()) {
        Toast.makeText(this, "Please fill
in all fields", Toast.LENGTH_SHORT).show()
    } else {
        Toast.makeText(this,          "Form
submitted                    successfully",
Toast.LENGTH_SHORT).show()
    }
}
```

- o This example validates the form when the button is clicked and shows a `Toast` message with feedback.

2. **Handling Other Events (Focus, Touch, Key Events)**: Besides clicks, Android supports other event handlers like `setOnFocusChangeListener`, `setOnTouchListener`, and `setOnKeyListener` to handle different types of user input.

Example (Focus Change):

149

```kotlin
val     editTextUsername:     EditText     =
findViewById(R.id.editTextUsername)
editTextUsername.setOnFocusChangeListener
{ _, hasFocus ->
    if (hasFocus) {
        editTextUsername.setHint("Enter
your username")
    } else {

editTextUsername.setHint("Username")
    }
}
```

o   This code changes the hint text in an `EditText`
    view based on whether the view has focus or not.

Using Checkboxes, RadioButtons, and Switches Effectively

1. **Checkboxes**: A **Checkbox** allows the user to select one
    or more options from a list. You can handle user input by
    checking the state of a checkbox.

    Example:

    ```kotlin
    ```

```kotlin
val      checkboxTerms:      CheckBox      =
findViewById(R.id.checkboxTerms)
checkboxTerms.setOnCheckedChangeListener {
_, isChecked ->
    if (isChecked) {
        Toast.makeText(this,  "Terms  and
Conditions                    accepted",
Toast.LENGTH_SHORT).show()
    } else {
        Toast.makeText(this,  "Terms  and
Conditions        not        accepted",
Toast.LENGTH_SHORT).show()
    }
}
```

- o The `setOnCheckedChangeListener` method is used to handle changes in the state of the checkbox. The lambda expression gets triggered whenever the checkbox is checked or unchecked.

2. **RadioButtons**: A **RadioButton** allows the user to choose one option from a group. Typically, radio buttons are grouped within a `RadioGroup`, which ensures that only one radio button can be selected at a time.

Example:

kotlin

151

```kotlin
val     radioGroup:     RadioGroup     =
findViewById(R.id.radioGroup)
radioGroup.setOnCheckedChangeListener { _,
checkedId ->
    val selectedOption = when (checkedId)
{
        R.id.radioOption1 -> "Option 1"
        R.id.radioOption2 -> "Option 2"
        else -> "Unknown"
    }
    Toast.makeText(this,     "Selected:
$selectedOption",
Toast.LENGTH_SHORT).show()
}
```

- o The `setOnCheckedChangeListener` is used to detect which radio button was selected, and based on the selected `checkedId`, we display the corresponding option.

3. **Switches**: A **Switch** is used to toggle between two options (e.g., ON/OFF or YES/NO).

Example:

```
kotlin
```

```kotlin
val     switchNotifications:     Switch     =
findViewById(R.id.switchNotifications)
```

```
switchNotifications.setOnCheckedChangeLis
tener { _, isChecked ->
    if (isChecked) {
        Toast.makeText(this,
"Notifications                     enabled",
Toast.LENGTH_SHORT).show()
    } else {
        Toast.makeText(this,
"Notifications                     disabled",
Toast.LENGTH_SHORT).show()
    }
}
```

  o The `setOnCheckedChangeListener` for the `Switch` will let you know whether it has been toggled on or off, and you can respond accordingly, such as enabling or disabling notifications.

Key Takeaways

- **Form Validation**: Ensure the data entered by users is correct using `TextWatcher` and other validation techniques to provide real-time feedback or upon form submission.

- **Event Handling**: Use `onClickListener` and other event handlers like `setOnFocusChangeListener`, `setOnTouchListener`, and `setOnKeyListener` to capture and respond to different types of user input.

- **Checkboxes, RadioButtons, and Switches**: These interactive UI elements allow users to make selections or toggle between options. Handling their states effectively with listeners enables smooth and intuitive user experiences.

In the next chapters, we will continue exploring more advanced techniques for handling user input and optimizing the user experience in Android apps.

CHAPTER 14

BUILDING AND USING APIS IN KOTLIN

In this chapter, we will learn how to build and use **APIs** in Kotlin. APIs (Application Programming Interfaces) allow different applications or services to communicate with each other. You can create your own APIs using Kotlin and also integrate third-party APIs into your Android applications. We will go through the steps of creating a simple API, integrating third-party libraries, handling data responses, and using APIs in Android apps.

Creating a Simple API with Kotlin

To create an API, you'll typically build a **backend service** that can handle requests from clients (such as your Android app). In this section, we will create a simple RESTful API using **Ktor**, a Kotlin-based framework for building server-side applications.

1. **Setting Up Ktor for API Development**: First, you need to add the Ktor dependencies in your `build.gradle` file.

   ```
   gradle
   ```

```
dependencies {
    implementation    "io.ktor:ktor-server-
core:1.6.0"
    implementation    "io.ktor:ktor-server-
netty:1.6.0"
    implementation         "io.ktor:ktor-
jackson:1.6.0"
    implementation
"org.jetbrains.kotlin:kotlin-
stdlib:1.5.21"
}
```

Ktor is lightweight and flexible, making it an excellent choice for building APIs in Kotlin.

2. **Building a Simple API Endpoint**: You can create an API endpoint using Ktor's routing system. Here's how you can create a simple GET endpoint that returns a message:

```
kotlin
```

```
import io.ktor.application.*
import io.ktor.features.ContentNegotiation
import io.ktor.http.HttpStatusCode
import io.ktor.jackson.jackson
import io.ktor.request.receive
import io.ktor.response.respond
import io.ktor.routing.*
```

```
import
io.ktor.server.engine.embeddedServer
import io.ktor.server.netty.Netty
import
io.ktor.server.plugins.statuspages.Status
Pages

data class Greeting(val message: String)

fun Application.module() {
    install(ContentNegotiation) {
        jackson { }
    }

    routing {
        get("/greeting") {
            call.respond(Greeting("Hello,
World!"))
        }

        post("/greeting") {
            val        greeting        =
call.receive<Greeting>()

call.respond(HttpStatusCode.Created,
greeting)
        }
    }
}
```

```
fun main() {
    embeddedServer(Netty, port = 8080,
module = Application::module).start(wait =
true)
}
```

- o **/greeting**: This is the GET endpoint that returns a simple greeting.
- o **POST Request**: It accepts a `Greeting` object and responds with the same object.

3. **Running the API**: To run the API, use the `embeddedServer` method. This creates a simple HTTP server running on port 8080. You can test the API by making GET and POST requests to `http://localhost:8080/greeting`.

Integrating Third-Party Libraries

Kotlin is compatible with a wide variety of third-party libraries that can help enhance your app's functionality. When working with APIs, libraries like **Retrofit**, **Ktor**, **Moshi**, and **Gson** are popular choices for making network requests and handling responses.

1. **Using Retrofit**: Retrofit is a powerful HTTP client for Android and Java, which simplifies making network

requests to a RESTful API. Retrofit abstracts the underlying HTTP request process and converts JSON responses into Kotlin data classes.

Setting Up Retrofit: Add the following dependencies to your `build.gradle` file:

```gradle
gradle
```

```gradle
dependencies {
    implementation
"com.squareup.retrofit2:retrofit:2.9.0"
    implementation
"com.squareup.retrofit2:converter-
gson:2.9.0"
}
```

2. **Creating a Retrofit Service**: Define your API endpoints using Retrofit's `@GET`, `@POST`, etc., annotations.

```kotlin
kotlin
```

```kotlin
interface ApiService {
    @GET("greeting")
    suspend fun getGreeting(): Greeting

    @POST("greeting")
    suspend      fun      postGreeting(@Body
greeting: Greeting): Response<Greeting>
```

159

```
}
```

3. **Initializing Retrofit**: Initialize Retrofit with a base URL and a converter to handle JSON responses (Gson, Moshi, etc.).

```kotlin
val retrofit = Retrofit.Builder()
    .baseUrl("http://localhost:8080/")  //
Base URL of the API

.addConverterFactory(GsonConverterFactory
.create())
    .build()

val              apiService           =
retrofit.create(ApiService::class.java)
```

Retrofit allows you to define your API calls as Kotlin suspending functions, making them simple to use in Kotlin's coroutines.

Handling Data Responses with Kotlin

Once you've set up your API service, you need to handle the data that is returned from the API, typically in the form of JSON. JSON responses can be parsed and mapped to Kotlin data classes.

160

1. **Creating Data Classes**: Define Kotlin data classes to represent the response data. For example, a `Greeting` class:

```kotlin
data class Greeting(
    val message: String
)
```

2. **Making Network Requests**: You can now use your Retrofit service to make network requests and retrieve the data.

Example using Coroutines:

```kotlin
val              apiService              =
retrofit.create(ApiService::class.java)
CoroutineScope(Dispatchers.IO).launch {
    try {
        val       greetingResponse      =
apiService.getGreeting()
        withContext(Dispatchers.Main) {
            println("Greeting:
${greetingResponse.message}")
        }
    } catch (e: Exception) {
```

161

```
withContext(Dispatchers.Main) {
    println("Error: ${e.message}")
}
    }
}
```

In this example:

- o The network request is executed on the IO dispatcher to avoid blocking the main thread.
- o The result is then posted to the main thread (Dispatchers.Main) to update the UI or handle the response.

3. **Handling Errors**: You can catch exceptions or handle errors, such as network issues, using a try-catch block. Additionally, Retrofit allows you to handle HTTP error responses using a Response object.

```
kotlin

val response = apiService.getGreeting()
if (response.isSuccessful) {
    val greeting = response.body()
    println("Greeting:
${greeting?.message}")
} else {
    println("Error: ${response.code()}")
}
```

This approach allows you to handle both successful and failed responses properly.

Creating APIs for Android Apps

When creating APIs for Android apps, you generally focus on building the backend API (for instance, using **Ktor**, **Spring Boot**, or **Node.js**) that serves as the bridge between your Android app and the data. Android acts as the client that sends requests to the server and handles the responses.

1. **Setting Up API Endpoints**: Define API endpoints on the server that the Android app will consume. These could be endpoints to fetch data (e.g., a list of users), create data (e.g., submit a form), or update data (e.g., edit a user profile).

2. **Android as a Client**: Use Retrofit, Ktor, or other HTTP clients to make requests to the server. As shown earlier, Retrofit is commonly used for Android development because of its ease of use, support for coroutines, and JSON parsing.

3. **Authentication and Security**: If your API requires authentication (e.g., via OAuth or API tokens), you can use headers or authentication interceptors with Retrofit to securely pass credentials.

Example (Adding an Authentication Token to Requests):

```kotlin
val interceptor = Interceptor { chain ->
    val         newRequest         =
chain.request().newBuilder()
        .addHeader("Authorization",
"Bearer $authToken")
        .build()
    chain.proceed(newRequest)
}

val okHttpClient = OkHttpClient.Builder()
    .addInterceptor(interceptor)
    .build()

val retrofit = Retrofit.Builder()
    .baseUrl("https://api.example.com/")
    .client(okHttpClient)

.addConverterFactory(GsonConverterFactory
.create())
    .build()
```

- o This example shows how to add an authentication token to every request made by Retrofit.

Key Takeaways

- **Building APIs with Kotlin**: You can create APIs using frameworks like Ktor or Spring Boot, which allow you to easily define endpoints and handle HTTP requests and responses.

- **Using Retrofit**: Retrofit simplifies the process of interacting with RESTful APIs in Android by providing an easy-to-use API for making network requests and handling responses.

- **Handling Responses**: In Kotlin, you can parse JSON responses from APIs into data classes using Retrofit and handle errors and responses using coroutines for asynchronous operations.

- **Creating APIs for Android Apps**: Android apps act as clients that communicate with backend APIs. By using libraries like Retrofit, you can send requests to APIs and handle responses easily and efficiently.

In the next chapters, we will continue exploring advanced techniques for integrating and optimizing API usage in Android apps, including handling complex data structures and improving network performance.

CHAPTER 15

TESTING KOTLIN CODE

In this chapter, we will explore **testing** in Kotlin, an essential part of building robust applications. We'll look at **unit testing**, **writing tests for Android apps**, **UI testing with Espresso**, and introduce the concept of **test-driven development (TDD)** in Kotlin. Testing ensures that your code works as expected, improves the quality of your app, and helps catch bugs early in the development process.

Unit Testing with JUnit

Unit testing is a type of testing that focuses on testing individual units of code, such as functions or methods. It ensures that each part of the code behaves correctly in isolation. In Kotlin, the most commonly used framework for unit testing is **JUnit**.

1. **Setting Up JUnit**: Add the JUnit dependency in your build.gradle file:

```gradle
dependencies {
    testImplementation "junit:junit:4.13.2"
```

```
    testImplementation
"org.jetbrains.kotlin:kotlin-test-
junit:1.5.21"
}
```

2. **Creating Unit Tests**: A basic unit test checks the functionality of a function or method. Here's how to write a simple unit test for a function in Kotlin using JUnit.

   Example:

```kotlin
import org.junit.Assert.*
import org.junit.Test

class CalculatorTest {

    @Test
    fun testAddition() {
        val result = add(2, 3)
        assertEquals(5, result)
    }

    fun add(a: Int, b: Int): Int {
        return a + b
    }
}
```

167

- o **@Test** annotation tells JUnit that the method should be executed as a test.
- o **assertEquals()** checks if the expected result matches the actual result.

3. **Running Unit Tests**: Unit tests can be run using the Android Studio test runner or the command line with Gradle. In Android Studio, right-click the test method or class and select **Run 'test'** to execute the tests.

Writing Tests for Android Apps

Writing tests for Android apps ensures that individual components, such as activities, fragments, and ViewModels, work as expected. Android provides tools like **JUnit** and **Mockito** for unit testing, and **Espresso** for UI testing.

1. **Testing ViewModels**: ViewModels are a crucial part of the Android architecture, and testing them ensures that the logic is functioning correctly. Here's how to write a simple unit test for a ViewModel.

Example:

```kotlin

class MyViewModel : ViewModel() {
```

```kotlin
    private        val        _text        =
MutableLiveData<String>()
    val  text:  LiveData<String>  get()  =
_text

    fun setText(value: String) {
        _text.value = value
    }
}

class MyViewModelTest {

    private   lateinit   var   viewModel:
MyViewModel

    @Before
    fun setUp() {
        viewModel = MyViewModel()
    }

    @Test
    fun testSetText() {
        viewModel.setText("Hello")
        assertEquals("Hello",
viewModel.text.value)
    }
}
```

- ○ **LiveData** is used to observe changes in the data. The test checks whether the `setText` function updates the `LiveData` value.
- ○ **@Before** annotation ensures the `viewModel` is set up before each test.

2. **Testing Activities and Fragments**: You can use **Mockito** to mock dependencies and test activities and fragments.

Example:

```kotlin
@Test
fun testActivityLaunch() {
    val               activity               =
Robolectric.buildActivity(MainActivity::c
lass.java).create().get()
    assertNotNull(activity)
}
```

- ○ **Robolectric** is a library that allows you to run Android tests outside the Android device or emulator.

Using Espresso for UI Testing

Espresso is a powerful UI testing framework for Android. It allows you to simulate user interactions and verify that the app's UI behaves as expected. Espresso tests run on an Android device or emulator, and they help verify that the UI elements display and behave correctly.

1. **Setting Up Espresso**: Add the necessary dependencies in your `build.gradle` file.

```gradle
dependencies {
    androidTestImplementation
"androidx.test.espresso:espresso-
core:3.4.0"
    androidTestImplementation
"androidx.test.ext:junit:1.1.3"
    androidTestImplementation
"androidx.test:runner:1.4.0"
}
```

2. **Writing Espresso Tests**: Espresso tests allow you to simulate user actions, such as clicking buttons, typing text, or checking if elements are visible.

Example:

```kotlin
@RunWith(AndroidJUnit4::class)
class MainActivityTest {

    @Test
    fun testButtonClick() {
        // Launch the activity
        val scenario = launchActivity<MainActivity>()

        // Perform a click on the button
        onView(withId(R.id.button))
            .perform(click())

        // Verify that the TextView
contains the expected text
        onView(withId(R.id.textView))

.check(matches(withText("Button
clicked!")))
    }
}
```

- o **onView(withId(...))** locates the UI element (in this case, the button or text view).
- o **perform(click())** simulates a click on the button.

o **check(matches(withText(...)))** verifies that the text in the `TextView` matches the expected value.

3. **Handling UI Synchronization**: Espresso automatically waits for UI elements to become visible or interactable before performing actions. However, for longer-running tasks (such as network calls), you can use `IdlingResource` to synchronize your tests.

Example:

kotlin

```
@Test
fun testAsyncTask() {
    onView(withId(R.id.button))
        .perform(click())

    // Wait until the task finishes
    Espresso.onIdle()

    onView(withId(R.id.textView))
        .check(matches(withText("Task
Completed")))
}
```

Test-Driven Development (TDD) with Kotlin

Test-driven development (TDD) is a software development process in which you write tests before writing the actual code. TDD promotes cleaner code and better software design. In TDD, the cycle typically follows these steps:

1. **Write a test**: Write a test for a new feature or function.
2. **Run the test**: Run the test and see it fail (since the feature is not yet implemented).
3. **Write code**: Write just enough code to pass the test.
4. **Refactor**: Refactor the code, making improvements while ensuring the test still passes.
5. **Repeat**: Repeat the cycle for each new feature or change.
6. **Example of TDD Cycle**:
   o **Step 1**: Write a failing test.

kotlin

```
@Test
fun testAddition() {
    val result = add(2, 3)
    assertEquals(5, result)
}
```

   o **Step 2**: Write the minimal code to make the test pass.

174

```kotlin
fun add(a: Int, b: Int): Int {
    return a + b
}
```

- o **Step 3**: Refactor (if necessary) and ensure the test still passes.

7. **Advantages of TDD**:
   - o Ensures code correctness from the start.
   - o Helps with better software design by focusing on testable units.
   - o Reduces the likelihood of bugs.
   - o Provides a safety net for future changes and refactoring.

Key Takeaways

- **Unit Testing with JUnit**: JUnit is a popular testing framework for Kotlin, allowing you to test individual units of code and ensure they work as expected.
- **Writing Tests for Android Apps**: You can write unit tests for Android components like ViewModels and Activities using tools like **JUnit** and **Mockito**.

- **Espresso for UI Testing**: Espresso simplifies UI testing by simulating user interactions and verifying UI behavior, ensuring that your app's interface works as intended.

- **Test-Driven Development (TDD)**: TDD encourages writing tests before the code, promoting clean, maintainable, and bug-free software.

In the next chapters, we will continue exploring advanced testing techniques and best practices for building high-quality Kotlin and Android applications.

CHAPTER 16

WORKING WITH ANDROID LIFECYCLE

In this chapter, we'll dive into the **Android lifecycle**, specifically focusing on **Activity** and **Fragment** lifecycles. Understanding the lifecycle of these components is essential for building efficient and responsive Android applications. We'll also cover how to manage resources during lifecycle changes and how to save and restore **instance state** to handle configuration changes like device rotations.

Understanding the Android Activity and Fragment Lifecycle

The **Activity** and **Fragment** lifecycles are at the core of Android's component management system. Understanding when and why components are created, paused, resumed, and destroyed is crucial for building apps that behave predictably and efficiently.

Activity Lifecycle

An **Activity** represents a single screen in an app. It goes through several stages during its lifetime. The most common lifecycle methods are:

1. **onCreate()**: This is called when the Activity is first created. This is where you initialize your app, set up the UI, and prepare any resources.

```kotlin
override fun onCreate(savedInstanceState:
Bundle?) {
    super.onCreate(savedInstanceState)

setContentView(R.layout.activity_main)
}
```

2. **onStart()**: Called after onCreate() or when the activity is becoming visible to the user.

```kotlin
override fun onStart() {
    super.onStart()
}
```

3. **onResume()**: This is called when the activity comes to the foreground and the user can interact with it. It's the best place to start animations or resume ongoing tasks.

```kotlin
override fun onResume() {
```

```kotlin
    super.onResume()
}
```

4. **onPause()**: Called when the activity is partially obscured (e.g., another activity comes in front of it). Use this method to pause or adjust resources (e.g., stop animations, save data).

   kotlin

```kotlin
override fun onPause() {
    super.onPause()
}
```

5. **onStop()**: Called when the activity is no longer visible. Use this method to release resources or save data.

   kotlin

```kotlin
override fun onStop() {
    super.onStop()
}
```

6. **onRestart()**: Called when the activity is coming back to the foreground after being stopped.

   kotlin

```kotlin
override fun onRestart() {
    super.onRestart()
```

```
}
```

7. **onDestroy()**: This method is called when the activity is being destroyed. You can use this to release any resources that were tied to the activity.

kotlin

```
override fun onDestroy() {
    super.onDestroy()
}
```

Fragment Lifecycle

Fragments are a part of the **Activity** lifecycle but have their own lifecycle methods. The Fragment lifecycle is tied to the **Activity** lifecycle, but they can have their own set of methods.

1. **onAttach()**: This is called when a fragment is first attached to its activity.

kotlin

```
override fun onAttach(context: Context) {
    super.onAttach(context)
}
```

2. **onCreate()**: Called to initialize the fragment. This is where you can set up non-UI resources.

```
kotlin
```

```
override fun onCreate(savedInstanceState:
Bundle?) {
    super.onCreate(savedInstanceState)
}
```

3. **onCreateView()**: Called to inflate the fragment's UI. Here, you will typically return the view to be displayed.

```
kotlin
```

```
override fun onCreateView(
    inflater: LayoutInflater, container:
ViewGroup?,
    savedInstanceState: Bundle?
): View? {
    return
inflater.inflate(R.layout.fragment_sample
, container, false)
}
```

4. **onActivityCreated()**: This is called after onCreateView() and when the activity's onCreate() method has finished executing.

```
kotlin
```

```
override                        fun
onActivityCreated(savedInstanceState:
Bundle?) {

super.onActivityCreated(savedInstanceStat
e)
}
```

5. **onStart()** and **onResume()**: Similar to the activity lifecycle, these methods are called when the fragment becomes visible or starts interacting with the user.

6. **onPause()**, **onStop()**, and **onDestroy()**: These methods are similar to their counterparts in the **Activity** lifecycle and are called when the fragment is no longer visible or is being destroyed.

Managing Resources During Lifecycle Changes

When activities or fragments are paused, stopped, or destroyed, it's essential to manage resources efficiently to avoid memory leaks and optimize app performance.

1. **Handling Background Tasks**: Long-running tasks like network calls or background services should be paused or stopped during the lifecycle changes. You can use **onPause()** or **onStop()** to cancel any ongoing tasks.

Example (Canceling a background task):

```kotlin
override fun onPause() {
    super.onPause()
    myAsyncTask.cancel(true)    // Cancel
the task when the activity is paused
}
```

2. **Releasing Resources**: Resources such as database connections, sensors, or network connections should be released when they are no longer needed.

Example (Releasing resources in `onStop()`):

```kotlin
override fun onStop() {
    super.onStop()
    database.close()    // Close database
when activity is not visible
}
```

3. **Handling Configuration Changes**: When the device is rotated, the system will destroy and recreate the activity by default. You can handle these changes by saving and restoring the **instance state** or by using `ViewModels`.

183

Saving Instance State

When an activity or fragment is destroyed and recreated (e.g., due to a configuration change like device rotation), you need to preserve the UI state, such as user inputs and UI elements. Android provides the `onSaveInstanceState()` method for saving simple data that can be restored when the activity or fragment is recreated.

1. **Saving Instance State**: Override the `onSaveInstanceState()` method to save data before the activity is destroyed.

   Example:

   ```kotlin
   override fun onSaveInstanceState(outState:
   Bundle) {
       super.onSaveInstanceState(outState)
       outState.putString("user_input",
   editText.text.toString())    // Save user
   input
   }
   ```

   o The `Bundle` object (`outState`) is used to store the state data.

184

2. **Restoring Instance State**: You can restore the state in onCreate() or onRestoreInstanceState() (called after onStart()).

Example:

```kotlin
override fun onCreate(savedInstanceState:
Bundle?) {
    super.onCreate(savedInstanceState)
    if (savedInstanceState != null) {
        val          userInput          =
savedInstanceState.getString("user_input"
)
        editText.setText(userInput)    //
Restore user input
    }
}
```

3. **Handling Fragment State**: In fragments, you can save and restore the state just like in activities.

Example (Fragment):

```kotlin
override fun onSaveInstanceState(outState:
Bundle) {
```

```
    super.onSaveInstanceState(outState)
    outState.putString("fragment_text",
textView.text.toString())  // Save data
}

override                          fun
onViewStateRestored(savedInstanceState:
Bundle?) {

super.onViewStateRestored(savedInstanceSt
ate)
    savedInstanceState?.let {
        val        restoredText      =
it.getString("fragment_text")
        textView.text = restoredText   //
Restore data
    }
}
```

Key Takeaways

- **Activity and Fragment Lifecycle**: Understanding the lifecycle of **Activity** and **Fragment** is crucial for managing UI components and resources correctly. Key lifecycle methods include onCreate(), onStart(), onResume(), onPause(), onStop(), and onDestroy().

- **Managing Resources**: It's essential to manage resources like background tasks, database connections, and sensors efficiently during lifecycle changes to prevent memory leaks and optimize performance.

- **Saving and Restoring State**: Use `onSaveInstanceState()` to save UI state (such as user input) before an activity or fragment is destroyed and `onRestoreInstanceState()` or `onCreate()` to restore the state when the activity or fragment is recreated.

- **Configuration Changes**: Handle configuration changes like device rotations by saving and restoring instance state, or by using `ViewModels` to maintain state across configuration changes.

In the next chapters, we will continue to explore more advanced Android lifecycle concepts and how to build apps that manage state and resources efficiently during lifecycle events.

CHAPTER 17

MULTITHREADING AND BACKGROUND TASKS

In this chapter, we will explore **multithreading** and handling **background tasks** in Android applications using Kotlin. Asynchronous processing is crucial for running time-consuming operations (like network calls, data processing, or database operations) without blocking the main UI thread. We'll cover traditional threading mechanisms like **AsyncTask**, **Handler**, and **Service**, as well as the modern approach with **Kotlin Coroutines**, which simplifies background task management.

Threading in Android with Kotlin

In Android, threading allows you to run operations on separate threads so that the UI thread (main thread) remains responsive. The main thread handles user interactions and UI updates, while background threads handle long-running operations.

1. **Creating a Basic Thread**: In Kotlin, you can create a new thread using the `Thread` class. This is a simple approach for creating background tasks.

188

Example:

```kotlin
val thread = Thread(Runnable {
    // Perform background task here
    println("Background task running in a
separate thread")
})
thread.start()
```

- o This creates a new thread and executes the code within the `Runnable` on that thread.

2. **Using `Runnable` with Thread**: `Runnable` is a functional interface in Kotlin used to define the task to be executed in the background.

Example:

```kotlin
val runnable = Runnable {
    // Perform background task
    println("Background task executed")
}
Thread(runnable).start()
```

189

Using AsyncTask, Handler, and Service

Before Kotlin coroutines became popular, Android developers commonly used **AsyncTask**, **Handler**, and **Service** for handling background tasks. While these methods are still used, they are less efficient and harder to manage compared to coroutines. However, understanding them is important for maintaining legacy apps.

1. **AsyncTask** (Deprecated in API Level 30): **AsyncTask** was used for performing background operations and updating the UI thread. It has been deprecated in favor of Kotlin coroutines and other APIs.

   Example:

```kotlin
class MyAsyncTask : AsyncTask<Void, Void, String>() {
    override fun doInBackground(vararg params: Void?): String {
        // Perform background work here
        return "Task Completed"
    }

    override fun onPostExecute(result: String?) {
        super.onPostExecute(result)
        // Update UI with result
```

```
Toast.makeText(applicationContext, result,
Toast.LENGTH_SHORT).show()
    }
}
```

```
MyAsyncTask().execute()
```

- o **doInBackground()** performs background work.
- o **onPostExecute()** is called after the background work completes, and it's used to update the UI.

2. **Handler**: A **Handler** is used to send and process messages or runnable tasks from a background thread to the main thread. This is useful for communicating between threads.

   Example:

   ```kotlin
   val              handler              =
   Handler(Looper.getMainLooper())

   Thread {
       // Background task
       Thread.sleep(2000)      //      Simulate
   background work
   ```

```kotlin
handler.post {
    // Code to execute on the main
thread

Toast.makeText(applicationContext,    "Task
completed", Toast.LENGTH_SHORT).show()
    }
}.start()
```

- o The **Handler** is initialized with the main thread's `Looper` (`Looper.getMainLooper()`), which allows it to execute tasks on the main thread.

3. **Service**: A **Service** is an Android component used for long-running background tasks. Services run in the background independently of the app's UI. You can use a **Service** for tasks like playing music, handling network calls, or processing data.

Example:

kotlin

```kotlin
class MyService : Service() {
    override fun onBind(intent: Intent?):
IBinder? {
        return null
    }
```

```
override   fun   onStartCommand(intent:
Intent?, flags: Int, startId: Int): Int {
    // Perform background task here
    return START_STICKY
}
}
```

o The **onStartCommand()** method is called when
   the service is started. This is where you put long-
   running tasks.

Working with Kotlin Coroutines for Background Tasks

Kotlin Coroutines provide a more efficient and easier-to-use
approach for managing background tasks in Android. Coroutines
allow you to write asynchronous code in a sequential manner,
making it easier to work with background tasks, UI updates, and
concurrency.

1. **Setting Up Coroutines**: To start using Kotlin coroutines,
   add the necessary dependencies to your `build.gradle`
   file.

```
gradle

dependencies {
```

```
    implementation
"org.jetbrains.kotlinx:kotlinx-
coroutines-android:1.5.2"
    implementation
"org.jetbrains.kotlinx:kotlinx-
coroutines-core:1.5.2"
}
```

2. **Basic Coroutine Setup**: You can launch coroutines using the `launch` function and specify which dispatcher the coroutine should run on. For example, the **Dispatchers.IO** dispatcher is used for background tasks such as network calls and database operations.

    Example:

```kotlin
// Run a background task in a coroutine
CoroutineScope(Dispatchers.IO).launch {
    // Perform background task here
    val result = fetchDataFromNetwork()

    // Switch to the main thread to update the UI
    withContext(Dispatchers.Main) {
        textView.text = result
    }
}
```

194

- o **Dispatchers.IO** is used for I/O-bound tasks.
- o **Dispatchers.Main** is used to update the UI on the main thread.

3. **Suspending Functions**: Kotlin's **suspending functions** allow you to write asynchronous code in a sequential style. A suspending function can be paused and resumed without blocking a thread.

Example (Suspending Function for Network Call):

```kotlin

suspend fun fetchDataFromNetwork(): String
{
    delay(2000)  // Simulate network delay
    return "Data fetched from network"
}
```

- o The **delay()** function is a non-blocking suspension point, allowing the coroutine to yield control to other tasks.
- o **suspend** functions can only be called within other coroutines or suspending functions.

4. **Handling Results with async and await**: The **async** coroutine builder allows you to perform multiple background tasks simultaneously and collect their results using **await()**.

195

Example (Using `async` and `await`):

```kotlin
val result1 = async(Dispatchers.IO) {
fetchDataFromNetwork() }
val result2 = async(Dispatchers.IO) {
fetchDataFromDatabase() }

// Wait for both results and update the UI
val resultData = "${result1.await()} -
${result2.await()}"
withContext(Dispatchers.Main) {
    textView.text = resultData
}
```

- o **async** allows concurrent execution of background tasks.
- o **await()** suspends the execution of the coroutine until the result is available.

5. **Handling Network Errors and Retries**: Kotlin coroutines provide a simple way to handle network errors and retries using **try-catch** blocks and **retry** mechanisms.

Example (Handling Errors and Retries):

```kotlin
```

```kotlin
suspend fun fetchDataWithRetry(): String {
    var attempt = 0
    val maxRetries = 3
    while (attempt < maxRetries) {
        try {
            // Simulate network call
            return fetchDataFromNetwork()
        } catch (e: Exception) {
            attempt++
            if (attempt == maxRetries)
throw e
            delay(1000) // Retry after a
short delay
        }
    }
    return "Failed to fetch data"
}
```

- o **try-catch** is used to handle errors.
- o **delay()** allows retrying the task after a short period.

Key Takeaways

- **Threading in Android**: Threads are used to run tasks in the background to keep the UI responsive. You can use

197

the `Thread` class or older mechanisms like **AsyncTask**, **Handler**, and **Service**.

- **Kotlin Coroutines**: Coroutines are a modern and efficient way to handle background tasks in Android. They provide a sequential programming model for asynchronous code, making it easier to work with network calls, database operations, and UI updates.

- **Using Coroutines for Background Tasks**: With `launch`, `async`, and `suspend` functions, Kotlin coroutines simplify working with background tasks and make asynchronous programming more intuitive.

- **Handling Errors and Retries**: Coroutines allow you to manage errors and implement retries with simple `try-catch` blocks and delays.

In the next chapters, we will explore advanced background task management techniques and how to integrate them into real-world Android apps.

CHAPTER 18

CREATING CUSTOM VIEWS IN ANDROID

In this chapter, we'll explore the process of creating **custom views** in Android. Custom views allow you to design unique and tailored UI components that cater to your app's specific needs. By creating custom views, you can extend the functionality of built-in views or design entirely new ones that better fit your design requirements. We will cover **designing custom UI components**, **handling custom drawing with Canvas**, and **implementing custom views** to meet your app's unique needs.

Designing Custom UI Components

A **custom view** in Android is a view that is created by extending one of Android's existing view classes (such as `View`, `TextView`, `ImageView`, etc.) to modify its appearance or behavior. You may create custom views when none of the standard Android widgets fit your needs, or when you want to create complex UI components that are not available by default.

1. **Basic Structure of a Custom View**:

- o **Inheriting from `View`**: The basic approach to creating a custom view is to extend the `View` class (or one of its subclasses).
- o **Constructor**: The constructor initializes the custom view.
- o **`onDraw()` Method**: This method is where the custom drawing happens. It's responsible for rendering the view's content.
- o **`onSizeChanged()` Method**: You can override this method to respond to changes in the view's size (e.g., when the view is resized).

Example:

```kotlin
kotlin


class CustomView(context: Context, attrs:
AttributeSet) : View(context, attrs) {

    init {
        // Initialize any attributes or
default behavior here
    }

    override fun onDraw(canvas: Canvas) {
        super.onDraw(canvas)
        // Custom drawing logic here
```

```
        canvas.drawColor(Color.RED)      //
Example: Draw a red background
    }

    override fun onSizeChanged(w: Int, h:
Int, oldW: Int, oldH: Int) {
        super.onSizeChanged(w,   h,   oldW,
oldH)
        // Handle size change, e.g., update
internal data
    }
}
```

In this example:

- o The CustomView class extends the View class and overrides the onDraw() method to perform custom drawing.
- o The onSizeChanged() method is used to handle changes in the view's size.

2. **Attributes and Customization**: You can define custom XML attributes for your custom view. This allows you to modify its appearance and behavior directly from the XML layout file.

Example:

```
xml
```

```
<com.example.myapp.CustomView
    android:layout_width="match_parent"
    android:layout_height="200dp"

app:customColor="@color/colorPrimary"/>
```

Custom Attributes:

```kotlin
val              typedArray              =
context.obtainStyledAttributes(attrs,
R.styleable.CustomView)
val              customColor             =
typedArray.getColor(R.styleable.CustomVie
w_customColor, Color.BLACK)
typedArray.recycle()
```

- o In this example, `obtainStyledAttributes()` is used to read custom attributes from XML (such as a custom color). You define the custom attributes in `res/values/attrs.xml`.

Handling Custom Drawing with Canvas

One of the most powerful features of custom views is the ability to perform **custom drawing** using the **Canvas** class. The `onDraw()` method is where you will write custom code to draw shapes, text, images, or other elements.

1. **Using the Canvas Object**:
   - o The `Canvas` object in the `onDraw()` method allows you to perform all types of drawing.
   - o You can draw shapes like rectangles, circles, and paths, and even use custom paint styles to define how the elements should look (e.g., color, stroke width).

Example (Drawing a Circle):

```kotlin
override fun onDraw(canvas: Canvas) {
    super.onDraw(canvas)

    val paint = Paint()
    paint.color = Color.BLUE
    paint.strokeWidth = 5f
    paint.style = Paint.Style.FILL

    val radius = 100f
    val x = width / 2f
    val y = height / 2f

    canvas.drawCircle(x, y, radius, paint)
}
```

- o In this example, we use the `Canvas.drawCircle()` method to draw a circle at the center of the view.
- o The **Paint** object defines the color and style (filled circle).

2. **Drawing Other Shapes**: You can draw other shapes (e.g., rectangles, lines, paths) using the respective `Canvas` methods.

Example (Drawing a Rectangle):

kotlin

```
override fun onDraw(canvas: Canvas) {
    super.onDraw(canvas)

    val paint = Paint()
    paint.color = Color.GREEN
    paint.style = Paint.Style.FILL

    val rect = Rect(50, 50, 300, 300)
    canvas.drawRect(rect, paint)
}
```

Example (Drawing Text):

kotlin

```
override fun onDraw(canvas: Canvas) {
```

```
super.onDraw(canvas)

val paint = Paint()
paint.color = Color.BLACK
paint.textSize = 50f

canvas.drawText("Hello, Custom View!",
50f, 100f, paint)
}
```

o **drawText()** is used to draw text on the canvas with a specific `Paint` object that determines the text's appearance (e.g., color, size).

Implementing Custom Views for Your App's Needs

Custom views in Android are typically used when the built-in UI components (like `Button`, `TextView`, or `ImageView`) don't meet your requirements. By creating custom views, you can design complex and interactive UI elements that match your app's unique style.

1. **Custom ProgressBar**: You can create a custom progress bar that fits the app's design, such as a circular progress indicator or a progress bar with a custom shape.

   Example (Custom Circular Progress Bar):

```kotlin
kotlin

class CircularProgressBar(context:
Context, attrs: AttributeSet) :
View(context, attrs) {
    private val paint = Paint()

    override fun onDraw(canvas: Canvas) {
        super.onDraw(canvas)

        val width = width.toFloat()
        val height = height.toFloat()
        val radius = Math.min(width,
height) / 2f
        val cx = width / 2f
        val cy = height / 2f

        // Draw a circular background
        paint.color = Color.GRAY
        paint.style = Paint.Style.STROKE
        paint.strokeWidth = 20f
        canvas.drawCircle(cx, cy, radius,
paint)

        // Draw a circular progress
        paint.color = Color.BLUE
        paint.strokeCap = Paint.Cap.ROUND
        val angle = 270f  // Represents the
progress (e.g., 270 degrees for 75%)
```

```
        canvas.drawArc(cx - radius, cy -
radius, cx + radius, cy + radius, -90f,
angle, false, paint)
    }
}
```

- o This custom view draws a circular progress indicator, allowing you to visually represent progress in your app.

2. **Custom Button with Icon and Text**: You can create a button that combines both an image and text to create a more unique interactive element.

Example:

kotlin

```
class IconButton(context: Context, attrs:
AttributeSet) : Button(context, attrs) {

    private  val  icon:  Drawable  =
resources.getDrawable(R.drawable.icon)

    override fun onDraw(canvas: Canvas) {
        super.onDraw(canvas)

        // Draw the icon and text
        icon.setBounds(0, 0, 50, 50)
        icon.draw(canvas)
```

```
        val textPaint = Paint()
        textPaint.color = Color.BLACK
        textPaint.textSize = 40f
        canvas.drawText("Custom    Button",
60f, height / 2f, textPaint)
    }
}
```

- o This custom button draws an icon and text within a single view.

3. **Custom Views for Interactivity**: Custom views can be made interactive by handling touch events, such as dragging, clicking, or swiping.

Example (Detecting Touch Event):

```
kotlin


override     fun     onTouchEvent(event:
MotionEvent): Boolean {
    if         (event.action         ==
MotionEvent.ACTION_DOWN) {
        // Handle touch event (e.g., change
color)
        paint.color = Color.RED
        invalidate()  // Redraw  the  view
with updated state
        return true
```

```
    }
    return super.onTouchEvent(event)
}
```

- o **onTouchEvent()** handles touch interactions, and **invalidate()** triggers a redraw of the view with the updated state.

Key Takeaways

- **Custom Views**: Create custom views by extending the `View` class and overriding methods like `onDraw()`, `onSizeChanged()`, and others to handle drawing and layout behavior.
- **Canvas and Custom Drawing**: Use the `Canvas` object in the `onDraw()` method to draw shapes, text, or other UI elements, and use the `Paint` object to style the drawing.
- **Custom Components**: You can create interactive and highly customized UI components (e.g., progress bars, buttons) by designing them from scratch.
- **Handling User Interactions**: Custom views can handle touch events to allow interaction with users, enabling you to create dynamic and responsive UI components.

In the next chapters, we will continue exploring advanced custom view techniques and how to optimize the performance and usability of your custom components in Android apps.

CHAPTER 19

DEBUGGING AND ERROR HANDLING IN KOTLIN

In this chapter, we will focus on **debugging** and **error handling** in Kotlin, both of which are essential skills for building robust and reliable applications. We will cover how to use **Logcat** for debugging, how to handle errors with **try-catch** blocks, and follow **best practices** for managing errors in Kotlin to ensure that your app performs well and provides a good user experience.

Using Logcat for Debugging

Logcat is a powerful tool built into Android Studio that allows you to view system logs, which include important information about your app's execution, warnings, errors, and other output. Logcat is essential for identifying issues and debugging code.

1. **Logcat Basics**: Logcat displays messages logged with the `Log` class in Android. You can log messages at different levels: **Verbose**, **Debug**, **Info**, **Warn**, **Error**, and **Assert**. The messages are visible in the **Logcat window** in Android Studio.

2. **Logging in Kotlin**: You can use the `Log` class to write messages to the Logcat console. Here's an example of how to log messages in Kotlin:

```kotlin

import android.util.Log

class MyActivity : AppCompatActivity() {

    override                              fun
    onCreate(savedInstanceState: Bundle?) {

    super.onCreate(savedInstanceState)

    setContentView(R.layout.activity_main)

        Log.v("MyActivity",   "This   is   a
    VERBOSE log message.")
        Log.d("MyActivity",   "This   is   a
    DEBUG log message.")
        Log.i("MyActivity",   "This   is   an
    INFO log message.")
        Log.w("MyActivity",   "This   is   a
    WARN log message.")
        Log.e("MyActivity",   "This   is   an
    ERROR log message.")
    }
}
```

- o **Log.v()**: Verbose log for detailed debugging.
- o **Log.d()**: Debug log for general debugging.
- o **Log.i()**: Info log for informative messages.
- o **Log.w()**: Warning log for potential issues.
- o **Log.e()**: Error log for errors or exceptions.

3. **Filtering Logs in Logcat**: You can filter logs by log level, tag, or message content in Logcat. This helps narrow down the logs to focus on what's relevant. For example:

    - o Use the search bar in Logcat to search for specific tags, like `MyActivity`.
    - o Use **Log levels** to filter for specific types of logs (e.g., show only errors).

4. **Logging Objects**: If you want to log an object's state, you can use **Log.d()** along with the **toString()** method of the object:

```kotlin
kotlin

val user = User("John", 30)
Log.d("UserInfo", user.toString())
```

Or, if you want to log complex objects, you can override the `toString()` method in your custom classes to provide meaningful log messages.

213

Error Handling with try-catch

Error handling is essential for ensuring that your application can gracefully handle unexpected situations, such as network errors, invalid input, or unexpected data.

1. **Basic try-catch Block**: In Kotlin, **try-catch** blocks are used to handle exceptions. Here's a basic example:

```kotlin
kotlin

try {
    val result = 10 / 0 // This will throw
an ArithmeticException
} catch (e: ArithmeticException) {
    Log.e("ErrorHandling",         "Error:
${e.message}")
}
```

   o **try**: The block of code that may throw an exception.
   o **catch**: The block of code that handles the exception. It can catch specific exceptions and handle them.

2. **Catching Multiple Exceptions**: You can handle different exceptions in separate catch blocks, or you can use a single catch block to handle multiple exceptions.

214

Example (Multiple `catch` blocks):

```
kotlin

try {
    val input = "abc".toInt() // This will
throw NumberFormatException
} catch (e: NumberFormatException) {
    Log.e("ErrorHandling", "Invalid number
format")
} catch (e: Exception) {
    Log.e("ErrorHandling", "Unknown error:
${e.message}")
}
```

Example (Multiple exceptions in one block):

```
kotlin

try {
    // Some code that might throw
exceptions
} catch (e: IOException) {
    Log.e("ErrorHandling", "IOException
occurred")
} catch (e: IllegalArgumentException) {
    Log.e("ErrorHandling", "Invalid
argument")
}
```

3. **Using `finally` Block**: The `finally` block is optional and is always executed after the `try` and `catch` blocks, regardless of whether an exception was thrown or not. It's useful for cleanup operations.

```kotlin
try {
    val file = FileReader("somefile.txt")
} catch (e: IOException) {
    Log.e("ErrorHandling",    "File    not
found")
} finally {
    // Cleanup code (e.g., closing the file
or network connection)
    Log.d("ErrorHandling", "Finally block
executed")
}
```

4. **Throwing Exceptions**: You can manually throw exceptions using the `throw` keyword when you detect an error condition that requires stopping the current operation.

```kotlin
throw    IllegalArgumentException("Invalid
argument provided")
```

o   This can be used when you want to enforce constraints or validation rules in your application.

Best Practices for Kotlin Error Management

Effective error management ensures that your app behaves predictably even when unexpected issues occur. Below are some best practices for error handling in Kotlin:

1. **Catch Specific Exceptions**: Always try to catch specific exceptions rather than using a generic `Exception` catch-all. This makes it easier to understand the type of error and respond accordingly.

```kotlin
try {
    val file = FileReader("data.txt")
} catch (e: FileNotFoundException) {
    // Handle the case where the file is
not found
} catch (e: IOException) {
    // Handle other I/O errors
}
```

2. **Avoid Silent Failures**: Avoid catching exceptions and doing nothing with them (i.e., "swallowing" the exception). This can lead to bugs that are difficult to

diagnose. If an error occurs, log it, and when appropriate, show the user a meaningful message.

kotlin

```
try {
    val result = someFunctionThatMayFail()
} catch (e: Exception) {
    Log.e("ErrorHandling",    "An    error
occurred: ${e.message}")
    // Optionally, show a user-friendly
message
}
```

3. **Graceful Error Recovery**: Provide users with options for recovering from errors, such as retrying a network operation or using default values. For example, when an API call fails, you might allow users to retry the operation.

kotlin

```
try {
    val result = networkRequest()
} catch (e: Exception) {
    showRetryButton()
}
```

4. **Use Sealed Classes for Error Types**: Instead of using plain exceptions, you can define **sealed classes** to represent different error states. This can be useful for handling expected errors in a more controlled manner.

Example:

```kotlin
kotlin


sealed class NetworkResult {
    data class Success(val data: String) :
NetworkResult()
    data    class    Error(val    exception:
Exception) : NetworkResult()
}


fun makeNetworkRequest(): NetworkResult {
    return try {
        // Simulate successful network
response
        NetworkResult.Success("Data
fetched successfully")
    } catch (e: Exception) {
        NetworkResult.Error(e)
    }
}
```

o   This approach helps you manage errors in a more structured way, allowing you to handle both successes and failures in a single return type.

5. **Logging Errors**: Use **Logcat** for logging exceptions and errors. Always log error messages to provide detailed information for debugging.

Example:

kotlin

```
try {
    val result = fetchData()
} catch (e: Exception) {
    Log.e("ErrorHandling", "Error fetching
data: ${e.message}")
}
```

o   Include as much useful information as possible (e.g., error message, stack trace) in the logs to aid in debugging.

Key Takeaways

• **Logcat**: Use **Logcat** to log useful information and debug your app effectively. Log different log levels (Log.v(),

`Log.d()`, `Log.e()`, etc.) based on the importance of the message.

- **Error Handling with try-catch**: Use **try-catch** blocks to handle exceptions, catch specific errors, and ensure your app behaves gracefully even when errors occur.

- **Best Practices**: Catch specific exceptions, avoid silent failures, provide users with graceful error recovery options, and use **sealed classes** to model different error states.

- **Logging and Debugging**: Always log errors and important events to Logcat. Proper logging helps diagnose and resolve issues efficiently.

In the next chapters, we will continue exploring advanced debugging techniques and other best practices for building resilient and error-free Android applications.

CHAPTER 20

BUILDING A SIMPLE ANDROID APP (PART 1)

In this chapter, we will start the process of building a simple Android app from scratch. This is the first part of a multi-part series that will guide you through creating a fully functional app. In this chapter, we'll focus on planning the app, implementing the main structure and navigation, and creating the first screens of your app.

Planning the App (Requirements and Design)

Before you start writing code, it's important to plan your app. Proper planning helps ensure that your app is well-structured, user-friendly, and meets all necessary requirements. Let's break down the process into the following steps:

1. **Define the Purpose**: What problem does your app solve? What is the goal of the app? For this example, let's say we are building a **simple task manager** app that allows users to create, view, edit, and delete tasks.

2. **Identify the Features**: The core features of our task manager app might include:

    o **Create new tasks**.

    o **View all tasks**.

    o **Edit or delete tasks**.

    o **Mark tasks as completed**.

3. **Design the User Interface (UI)**: Create wireframes or mockups of the app's interface. For a simple task manager app, we could design the following screens:

    o **Home Screen**: Displays the list of tasks.

    o **Task Details Screen**: Shows details of a single task and allows the user to edit or delete it.

    o **Add/Edit Task Screen**: Allows the user to add or edit a task.

Tools like **Figma**, **Sketch**, or **Adobe XD** are great for UI/UX design, but for simplicity, we'll define the UI flow in code as we proceed.

4. **Decide on Navigation**: In our app, we will need to navigate between the following screens:

    o **Home Screen → Add/Edit Task Screen**: To create or edit tasks.

    o **Home Screen → Task Details Screen**: To view details of a task.

    o **Task Details Screen → Edit Task Screen**: To edit the task.

Implementing the Main Structure and Navigation

With the app's requirements and design in mind, we can now implement the app's main structure. We will use **Android's Navigation Component** to handle screen transitions, which simplifies the process of navigating between different screens.

1. **Setting Up Navigation Component**: To set up the navigation component, we need to add the following dependencies in our `build.gradle` file:

```gradle
gradle
```

```gradle
dependencies {
    implementation
"androidx.navigation:navigation-fragment-
ktx:2.3.5"
    implementation
"androidx.navigation:navigation-ui-
ktx:2.3.5"
}
```

2. **Defining Navigation Graph**: The **Navigation Graph** defines the possible paths between screens. We will create a navigation graph XML file to specify the app's navigation structure.

   o Right-click on the `res` folder in your project, and go to `New -> Android Resource File`.

- o Name the file `nav_graph.xml`, and set the **Resource Type** to **Navigation**.
- o Add the following content to the `nav_graph.xml` file:

xml

```xml
<?xml version="1.0" encoding="utf-8"?>
<navigation
xmlns:android="http://schemas.android.com
/apk/res/android"
    android:id="@+id/nav_graph"

app:startDestination="@id/homeFragment">

    <fragment
        android:id="@+id/homeFragment"

android:name="com.example.taskmanager.Hom
eFragment"
        android:label="Home"

app:destination="@id/addTaskFragment" />

    <fragment
        android:id="@+id/addTaskFragment"

android:name="com.example.taskmanager.Add
TaskFragment"
```

```
        android:label="Add Task" />

    <fragment

android:id="@+id/taskDetailFragment"

android:name="com.example.taskmanager.Tas
kDetailFragment"
        android:label="Task Detail" />
</navigation>
```

- o **startDestination** specifies the first screen (in this case, HomeFragment).
- o The fragments represent the different screens (Home, Add Task, and Task Detail).

3. **Creating Fragments**: Now, let's create the three main fragments:
   - o **HomeFragment**: Displays the list of tasks.
   - o **AddTaskFragment**: Allows the user to add or edit tasks.
   - o **TaskDetailFragment**: Shows the details of a selected task.

Creating the HomeFragment:

- o Right-click on the com.example.taskmanager package and create a new **Fragment** named HomeFragment.

226

- o In the `HomeFragment` layout XML file (`fragment_home.xml`), add a `RecyclerView` to display the list of tasks.

xml

```
<?xml version="1.0" encoding="utf-8"?>
<androidx.constraintlayout.widget.Constra
intLayout
xmlns:android="http://schemas.android.com
/apk/res/android"

xmlns:app="http://schemas.android.com/apk
/res-auto"

xmlns:tools="http://schemas.android.com/t
ools"
    android:layout_width="match_parent"
    android:layout_height="match_parent"
    tools:context=".HomeFragment">


<androidx.recyclerview.widget.RecyclerVie
w

android:id="@+id/recyclerViewTasks"

android:layout_width="match_parent"
```

```
android:layout_height="match_parent" />
</androidx.constraintlayout.widget.Constr
aintLayout>
```

- o The `RecyclerView` will display a list of tasks.
  We'll populate this RecyclerView later with the
  task data.

HomeFragment Code:

```
kotlin
```

```kotlin
class                HomeFragment          :
Fragment(R.layout.fragment_home) {
    override fun onViewCreated(view: View,
savedInstanceState: Bundle?) {
        super.onViewCreated(view,
savedInstanceState)

        // Set  up  the  RecyclerView  with
data
        val  recyclerView: RecyclerView  =
view.findViewById(R.id.recyclerViewTasks)
        recyclerView.layoutManager       =
LinearLayoutManager(context)

        // Dummy data
        val tasks = listOf("Task 1", "Task
2", "Task 3")
```

```
recyclerView.adapter                =
TaskAdapter(tasks)
    }
}
```

4. **Creating the AddTaskFragment**: Create a new fragment for adding or editing tasks. This fragment will contain form fields for entering task information, such as a title and description.

   AddTaskFragment Layout:

   xml

```
<?xml version="1.0" encoding="utf-8"?>
<androidx.constraintlayout.widget.Constra
intLayout
xmlns:android="http://schemas.android.com
/apk/res/android"

xmlns:app="http://schemas.android.com/apk
/res-auto"

xmlns:tools="http://schemas.android.com/t
ools"
    android:layout_width="match_parent"
    android:layout_height="match_parent"
    tools:context=".AddTaskFragment">
```

```
    <EditText

android:id="@+id/editTextTaskTitle"
        android:layout_width="0dp"

android:layout_height="wrap_content"
        android:hint="Task Title"
        android:layout_marginTop="16dp"

app:layout_constraintTop_toTopOf="parent"

app:layout_constraintStart_toStartOf="par
ent"

app:layout_constraintEnd_toEndOf="parent"
/>

    <Button
        android:id="@+id/buttonSaveTask"

android:layout_width="wrap_content"

android:layout_height="wrap_content"
        android:text="Save Task"

app:layout_constraintTop_toBottomOf="@id/
editTextTaskTitle"
```

```
app:layout_constraintStart_toStartOf="par
ent"

app:layout_constraintEnd_toEndOf="parent"
/>
</androidx.constraintlayout.widget.Constr
aintLayout>
```

AddTaskFragment Code:

```kotlin
kotlin

class            AddTaskFragment           :
Fragment(R.layout.fragment_add_task) {
    override fun onViewCreated(view: View,
savedInstanceState: Bundle?) {
        super.onViewCreated(view,
savedInstanceState)

        val   editTextTitle:   EditText   =
view.findViewById(R.id.editTextTaskTitle)
        val    buttonSave:    Button    =
view.findViewById(R.id.buttonSaveTask)

        buttonSave.setOnClickListener {
            // Save task logic
            val          title         =
editTextTitle.text.toString()
            if (title.isNotEmpty()) {
```

231

```
                    // Logic to save the task
                    Toast.makeText(context,
    "Task saved", Toast.LENGTH_SHORT).show()
                }
            }
        }
    }
```

Creating the First Screens of Your App

With the structure and navigation in place, we now have the basic screens implemented for the app.

1. **Set up the MainActivity**: The `MainActivity` will serve as the host for the fragments. Set up the navigation component in the `MainActivity`.

   MainActivity Layout:

   ```
   xml
   ```

   ```xml
   <?xml version="1.0" encoding="utf-8"?>
   <androidx.drawerlayout.widget.DrawerLayout
   xmlns:android="http://schemas.android.com
   /apk/res/android"

   xmlns:app="http://schemas.android.com/apk
   /res-auto"
   ```

```
xmlns:tools="http://schemas.android.com/t
ools"
    android:layout_width="match_parent"
    android:layout_height="match_parent"
    tools:context=".MainActivity">


<androidx.fragment.app.FragmentContainerV
iew

android:id="@+id/nav_host_fragment"

android:layout_width="match_parent"

android:layout_height="match_parent"
        app:defaultNavHost="true"

app:navGraph="@navigation/nav_graph" />
</androidx.drawerlayout.widget.DrawerLayo
ut>
```

MainActivity Code:

```
kotlin

class           MainActivity            :
AppCompatActivity(R.layout.activity_main)
{
```

```
override                        fun
onCreate(savedInstanceState: Bundle?) {

super.onCreate(savedInstanceState)

    val         navController      =
findNavController(R.id.nav_host_fragment)
    val      appBarConfiguration    =
AppBarConfiguration(navController.graph)

setupActionBarWithNavController(navContro
ller, appBarConfiguration)
    }
}
```

Key Takeaways

- **App Planning**: Begin by defining your app's requirements and designing its structure. Use wireframes or mockups to visualize the user interface.
- **Navigation**: Use the **Navigation Component** to manage screen transitions. Create a **navigation graph** and set up the appropriate fragments and actions.
- **Fragments**: Build the main UI components as fragments (e.g., HomeFragment, AddTaskFragment). Each fragment represents a part of the app's UI and handles specific tasks.

- **UI Layouts**: Use XML layout files to design the UI of each screen. You can use various UI components like `RecyclerView`, `EditText`, and `Button`.

In the next part of this series, we will explore how to populate the RecyclerView with real data, handle task persistence (e.g., saving tasks in a database), and implement additional features to enhance the app.

CHAPTER 21

BUILDING A SIMPLE ANDROID APP (PART 2)

In this chapter, we will continue building the simple Android app we started in **Part 1**. We will focus on **integrating features like data input and display**, **working with multiple screens** (Activities/Fragments), and **adding more interactivity with Kotlin**. This chapter will build on the foundation established in Part 1 and add more functionality to the app, making it interactive and user-friendly.

Integrating Features Like Data Input and Display

1. **Adding Task Data Input**: In Part 1, we created a basic `AddTaskFragment` where users can input a task title. Now, let's expand this to allow users to input additional information, such as a task description, due date, or priority.

    Add Task Fragment Layout (Updated):

    ```xml
    xml
    ```

```xml
<?xml version="1.0" encoding="utf-8"?>
<androidx.constraintlayout.widget.Constra
intLayout
xmlns:android="http://schemas.android.com
/apk/res/android"

xmlns:app="http://schemas.android.com/apk
/res-auto"

xmlns:tools="http://schemas.android.com/t
ools"
    android:layout_width="match_parent"
    android:layout_height="match_parent"
    tools:context=".AddTaskFragment">

    <EditText

android:id="@+id/editTextTaskTitle"
        android:layout_width="0dp"

android:layout_height="wrap_content"
        android:hint="Task Title"
        android:layout_marginTop="16dp"

app:layout_constraintTop_toTopOf="parent"

app:layout_constraintStart_toStartOf="par
ent"
```

```
app:layout_constraintEnd_toEndOf="parent"
/>

    <EditText

android:id="@+id/editTextTaskDescription"
        android:layout_width="0dp"

android:layout_height="wrap_content"
        android:hint="Task Description"

app:layout_constraintTop_toBottomOf="@id/
editTextTaskTitle"

app:layout_constraintStart_toStartOf="par
ent"

app:layout_constraintEnd_toEndOf="parent"
        android:layout_marginTop="16dp" />

    <Button
        android:id="@+id/buttonSaveTask"

android:layout_width="wrap_content"

android:layout_height="wrap_content"
        android:text="Save Task"
```

```
app:layout_constraintTop_toBottomOf="@id/
editTextTaskDescription"

app:layout_constraintStart_toStartOf="par
ent"

app:layout_constraintEnd_toEndOf="parent"
        android:layout_marginTop="16dp" />
</androidx.constraintlayout.widget.Constr
aintLayout>
```

- o We've added an `EditText` for the **task description** below the task title input.
- o The `Save Task` button allows the user to save the task information.

2. **Handling User Input**: In the `AddTaskFragment`, we handle the user input by reading the data entered in the `EditText` views when the button is clicked.

AddTaskFragment Code (Updated):

```
kotlin
```

```
class            AddTaskFragment            :
Fragment(R.layout.fragment_add_task) {
    override fun onViewCreated(view: View,
savedInstanceState: Bundle?) {
```

```kotlin
    super.onViewCreated(view,
savedInstanceState)

    val  editTextTitle:  EditText  =
view.findViewById(R.id.editTextTaskTitle)
    val editTextDescription: EditText
=
view.findViewById(R.id.editTextTaskDescri
ption)
    val    buttonSave:    Button    =
view.findViewById(R.id.buttonSaveTask)

    buttonSave.setOnClickListener {
        // Get the input values
        val        title        =
editTextTitle.text.toString()
        val    description    =
editTextDescription.text.toString()

        if  (title.isNotEmpty()  &&
description.isNotEmpty()) {
            // Logic to save the task
(e.g., in a ViewModel or database)
            Toast.makeText(context,
"Task saved", Toast.LENGTH_SHORT).show()
        } else {
            Toast.makeText(context,
"Please    fill    in    all    fields",
Toast.LENGTH_SHORT).show()
```

```
            }
         }
      }
}
```

     ○   **Input Validation**: We check if both the task title and description are provided before saving. If either is empty, we show a **Toast** informing the user to fill in the required fields.

3. **Displaying Data**: In the `HomeFragment`, we display the list of tasks. To make the app dynamic, we'll simulate the task list by using a `RecyclerView` and displaying the tasks added in the `AddTaskFragment`.

HomeFragment Layout:

xml

```
<?xml version="1.0" encoding="utf-8"?>
<androidx.constraintlayout.widget.Constra
intLayout
xmlns:android="http://schemas.android.com
/apk/res/android"

xmlns:app="http://schemas.android.com/apk
/res-auto"

xmlns:tools="http://schemas.android.com/t
ools"
```

241

```
android:layout_width="match_parent"
android:layout_height="match_parent"
tools:context=".HomeFragment">
```

```
<androidx.recyclerview.widget.RecyclerVie
w

android:id="@+id/recyclerViewTasks"

android:layout_width="match_parent"

android:layout_height="match_parent" />
</androidx.constraintlayout.widget.Constr
aintLayout>
```

o The RecyclerView will display the list of tasks.

HomeFragment Code (Updated):

```kotlin
class            HomeFragment          :
Fragment(R.layout.fragment_home) {
    private   lateinit   var   taskAdapter:
TaskAdapter

    override fun onViewCreated(view: View,
savedInstanceState: Bundle?) {
```

```
        super.onViewCreated(view,
savedInstanceState)

        val recyclerView: RecyclerView =
view.findViewById(R.id.recyclerViewTasks)
        recyclerView.layoutManager        =
LinearLayoutManager(context)

        // Dummy data
        val tasks = mutableListOf("Task
1", "Task 2", "Task 3")
        taskAdapter = TaskAdapter(tasks)
        recyclerView.adapter = taskAdapter
    }

    fun addTask(task: String) {
        taskAdapter.addTask(task)
    }
}
```

- o We use the **TaskAdapter** to display the list of tasks in the RecyclerView.
- o The **addTask()** method is used to add new tasks dynamically to the list.

243

Working with Multiple Screens (Activities/Fragments)

In Android, an app typically navigates between **multiple screens**, which are either **Activities** or **Fragments**. In our app, we have already set up fragments for handling the main screen (`HomeFragment`) and the task creation screen (`AddTaskFragment`).

1. **Navigating Between Screens**: We will use the **Navigation Component** to handle navigation between these fragments. When a user clicks on a task in the list, we'll navigate to a **TaskDetailFragment** to display the details of the selected task.

   Example (Navigating to Task Detail):

   ```kotlin
   kotlin


   taskAdapter.setOnItemClickListener { task
   ->
       val            action           =
   HomeFragmentDirections.actionHomeFragment
   ToTaskDetailFragment(task)
       findNavController().navigate(action)
   }
   ```

   o When a task is clicked, we use the **Navigation Component** to navigate to the

```
TaskDetailFragment          using          the
findNavController() method.
```

2. **Task Detail Fragment**: Create a new fragment for displaying task details.

    TaskDetailFragment Layout:

    xml

```xml
<?xml version="1.0" encoding="utf-8"?>
<androidx.constraintlayout.widget.Constra
intLayout
xmlns:android="http://schemas.android.com
/apk/res/android"

xmlns:app="http://schemas.android.com/apk
/res-auto"

xmlns:tools="http://schemas.android.com/t
ools"
    android:layout_width="match_parent"
    android:layout_height="match_parent"
    tools:context=".TaskDetailFragment">

    <TextView

android:id="@+id/textViewTaskDetails"

android:layout_width="wrap_content"
```

```
android:layout_height="wrap_content"
        android:text="Task Details"
        android:layout_marginTop="32dp"

app:layout_constraintTop_toTopOf="parent"

app:layout_constraintStart_toStartOf="par
ent"

app:layout_constraintEnd_toEndOf="parent"
/>
</androidx.constraintlayout.widget.Constr
aintLayout>
```

TaskDetailFragment Code:

```kotlin
class          TaskDetailFragment          :
Fragment(R.layout.fragment_task_detail) {
    override fun onViewCreated(view: View,
savedInstanceState: Bundle?) {
        super.onViewCreated(view,
savedInstanceState)

        val task = arguments?.let {

TaskDetailFragmentArgs.fromBundle(it).tas
k
```

```
        }

        val    textView:    TextView   =
view.findViewById(R.id.textViewTaskDetail
s)
        textView.text = task ?: "No task
details available"
    }
}
```

o   We retrieve the task details passed from the
    previous screen and display them in the
    TextView.

Adding More Interactivity with Kotlin

1. **Handling Button Clicks**: We added a button in the
   `AddTaskFragment` for saving tasks. You can add more
   interactivity by handling different user actions, like
   editing or **deleting tasks**. Each action can trigger changes
   in the UI, such as refreshing the list of tasks or navigating
   to another screen.
2. **RecyclerView Click Handling**: To make the
   `RecyclerView` interactive, we add an
   `OnItemClickListener` in the adapter to handle task
   item clicks, allowing users to view task details or perform
   actions such as editing or deleting tasks.

247

Key Takeaways

- **Data Input and Display**: We implemented input fields in the `AddTaskFragment` for users to input task details and validated user input before saving it.
- **Navigation**: We used the **Navigation Component** to navigate between different fragments in the app (e.g., from the home screen to the task detail screen).
- **Multiple Screens**: We worked with multiple fragments in the app, each representing a different screen (home, add task, task details).
- **Interactivity**: We added button clicks and RecyclerView item clicks to make the app more interactive, allowing users to create, view, and navigate tasks.

In the next part, we will continue building this app by implementing persistent storage (such as a database) to save tasks, enhancing the functionality, and improving the user experience.

CHAPTER 22

FIREBASE INTEGRATION IN ANDROID

In this chapter, we will integrate **Firebase** into our Android app to handle authentication, store data, and perform real-time operations. Firebase provides a suite of backend services that can significantly speed up app development, including **Firebase Authentication** for user login, and **Firebase Realtime Database** or **Firestore** for storing and retrieving data.

Setting Up Firebase in Your Project

1. **Create a Firebase Project**:
   o Go to the Firebase Console.
   o Click on **"Add Project"** and follow the steps to create a new Firebase project.

2. **Integrating Firebase with Your Android App**: To integrate Firebase into your app, follow these steps:
   o In the Firebase Console, select your project and click **"Add App"**.

- o Choose **Android** as the platform and provide your app's **package name** (the same as your Android app's package name).
- o Download the `google-services.json` file and add it to your Android project. Place it in the `app` directory.

Add Firebase SDK Dependencies: In your `build.gradle` files, you need to add the Firebase dependencies:

- o In the **project-level `build.gradle`**:

```gradle
buildscript {
    repositories {
        google()
    }
    dependencies {
        classpath
'com.google.gms:google-
services:4.3.8'
    }
}
```

- o In the **app-level `build.gradle`**:

```gradle
```

```
apply                        plugin:
'com.google.gms.google-services'

dependencies {
    implementation
'com.google.firebase:firebase-
auth:21.0.1'
    implementation
'com.google.firebase:firebase-
database:20.0.3'
    //   Add   other   Firebase
dependencies as needed
}
```

- o   Sync your project with Gradle.

3.   **Enable Firebase Authentication**:

- o   In the Firebase Console, go to **Authentication** and enable the sign-in methods you want to use (e.g., Email/Password, Google Sign-In).
- o   For this example, we will enable **Email/Password** authentication.

Using Firebase for Authentication

Firebase Authentication provides easy-to-use SDKs to authenticate users with various providers like email/password,

Google, Facebook, etc. In this section, we'll implement basic **Email/Password** authentication.

1. **Sign-Up and Login**: To authenticate users, we will create a simple **SignUp** and **Login** screen.

   SignUpFragment Layout (fragment_sign_up.xml):

   xml

   ```xml
   <?xml version="1.0" encoding="utf-8"?>
   <androidx.constraintlayout.widget.Constra
   intLayout
   xmlns:android="http://schemas.android.com
   /apk/res/android"
       android:layout_width="match_parent"
       android:layout_height="match_parent">

       <EditText
           android:id="@+id/editTextEmail"
           android:layout_width="0dp"

   android:layout_height="wrap_content"
           android:hint="Email"
           android:layout_marginTop="16dp"

   app:layout_constraintTop_toTopOf="parent"
   ```

```xml
app:layout_constraintStart_toStartOf="par
ent"

app:layout_constraintEnd_toEndOf="parent"
/>

    <EditText

android:id="@+id/editTextPassword"
        android:layout_width="0dp"

android:layout_height="wrap_content"
        android:hint="Password"
        android:layout_marginTop="16dp"

app:layout_constraintTop_toBottomOf="@id/
editTextEmail"

app:layout_constraintStart_toStartOf="par
ent"

app:layout_constraintEnd_toEndOf="parent"
/>

    <Button
        android:id="@+id/buttonSignUp"

android:layout_width="wrap_content"
```

```
android:layout_height="wrap_content"
        android:text="Sign Up"

app:layout_constraintTop_toBottomOf="@id/
editTextPassword"

app:layout_constraintStart_toStartOf="par
ent"

app:layout_constraintEnd_toEndOf="parent"
/>
</androidx.constraintlayout.widget.Constr
aintLayout>
```

SignUpFragment Code:

```kotlin
kotlin

class            SignUpFragment            :
Fragment(R.layout.fragment_sign_up) {
    override fun onViewCreated(view: View,
savedInstanceState: Bundle?) {
        super.onViewCreated(view,
savedInstanceState)


        val  editTextEmail:  EditText  =
view.findViewById(R.id.editTextEmail)
        val  editTextPassword:  EditText  =
view.findViewById(R.id.editTextPassword)
```

```kotlin
        val    buttonSignUp:    Button    =
view.findViewById(R.id.buttonSignUp)

        buttonSignUp.setOnClickListener {
            val            email            =
editTextEmail.text.toString()
            val          password          =
editTextPassword.text.toString()

            if    (email.isNotEmpty()    &&
password.isNotEmpty()) {

FirebaseAuth.getInstance().createUserWith
EmailAndPassword(email, password)

.addOnCompleteListener { task ->
                            if
(task.isSuccessful) {

Toast.makeText(context,    "User    Created
Successfully", Toast.LENGTH_SHORT).show()
                    } else {

Toast.makeText(context,              "Error:
${task.exception?.message}",
Toast.LENGTH_SHORT).show()
                    }
                }
            } else {
```

255

```
                    Toast.makeText(context,
"Please    enter    email    and    password",
Toast.LENGTH_SHORT).show()
                    }
              }
       }
}
```

- ○ **createUserWithEmailAndPassword()**: This method is used to create a new user with email and password. If successful, a new Firebase user is created.

2. **Login Fragment Layout** (fragment_login.xml):

```
xml
```

```
<?xml version="1.0" encoding="utf-8"?>
<androidx.constraintlayout.widget.Constra
intLayout
xmlns:android="http://schemas.android.com
/apk/res/android"
    android:layout_width="match_parent"
    android:layout_height="match_parent">

    <EditText

android:id="@+id/editTextEmailLogin"
        android:layout_width="0dp"
```

256

```
android:layout_height="wrap_content"
        android:hint="Email"
        android:layout_marginTop="16dp"

app:layout_constraintTop_toTopOf="parent"

app:layout_constraintStart_toStartOf="par
ent"

app:layout_constraintEnd_toEndOf="parent"
/>

    <EditText

android:id="@+id/editTextPasswordLogin"
        android:layout_width="0dp"

android:layout_height="wrap_content"
        android:hint="Password"
        android:layout_marginTop="16dp"

app:layout_constraintTop_toBottomOf="@id/
editTextEmailLogin"

app:layout_constraintStart_toStartOf="par
ent"
```

```xml
app:layout_constraintEnd_toEndOf="parent"
/>

    <Button
        android:id="@+id/buttonLogin"

android:layout_width="wrap_content"

android:layout_height="wrap_content"
        android:text="Log In"

app:layout_constraintTop_toBottomOf="@id/
editTextPasswordLogin"

app:layout_constraintStart_toStartOf="par
ent"

app:layout_constraintEnd_toEndOf="parent"
/>
</androidx.constraintlayout.widget.Constr
aintLayout>
```

LoginFragment Code:

```kotlin
kotlin

class              LoginFragment            :
Fragment(R.layout.fragment_login) {
```

```kotlin
override fun onViewCreated(view: View,
savedInstanceState: Bundle?) {
    super.onViewCreated(view,
savedInstanceState)

    val editTextEmail: EditText =
view.findViewById(R.id.editTextEmailLogin
)
    val editTextPassword: EditText =
view.findViewById(R.id.editTextPasswordLo
gin)
    val buttonLogin: Button =
view.findViewById(R.id.buttonLogin)

    buttonLogin.setOnClickListener {
        val email =
editTextEmail.text.toString()
        val password =
editTextPassword.text.toString()

        if (email.isNotEmpty() &&
password.isNotEmpty()) {

FirebaseAuth.getInstance().signInWithEmai
lAndPassword(email, password)

.addOnCompleteListener { task ->
                    if
(task.isSuccessful) {
```

```
Toast.makeText(context,              "Login
Successful", Toast.LENGTH_SHORT).show()
                         } else {

Toast.makeText(context,             "Error:
${task.exception?.message}",
Toast.LENGTH_SHORT).show()
                         }
                       }
               } else {
                  Toast.makeText(context,
"Please    enter    email    and    password",
Toast.LENGTH_SHORT).show()
                  }
               }
           }
}
```

- ○ **signInWithEmailAndPassword()**: This method allows users to log in with their email and password.

Storing and Retrieving Data from Firebase

Now that we've implemented authentication, we can store and retrieve data from Firebase's **Realtime Database** or **Firestore**. In this section, we will use **Realtime Database** to store tasks.

1. **Setting Up Realtime Database**:

   o In the Firebase Console, go to the **Realtime Database** section and click **Create Database**.

   o Set the **rules** to allow read and write permissions for testing (for production, you will need to define proper rules):

   ```json
   json

   {
     "rules": {
       ".read": "auth != null",
       ".write": "auth != null"
     }
   }
   ```

2. **Storing Data in Realtime Database**:

   o To save a task to the database, we will use the Firebase **DatabaseReference** to get a reference to the `tasks` node and add data.

   Example Code:

   ```kotlin
   kotlin

   val database = FirebaseDatabase.getInstance().reference
   val task = Task("Task 1", "Description of Task 1")
   ```

```
database.child("tasks").push().setValue(t
ask)
    .addOnCompleteListener { task ->
        if (task.isSuccessful) {
            Toast.makeText(context,   "Task
saved", Toast.LENGTH_SHORT).show()
        } else {
            Toast.makeText(context, "Error
saving task", Toast.LENGTH_SHORT).show()
        }
    }
```

- o **push()** creates a unique ID for each task, and **setValue()** stores the task in the database.

3. **Retrieving Data from Firebase**:
   - o To retrieve tasks from Firebase, we will query the tasks node and update the UI with the data.

Example Code:

```kotlin
database.child("tasks").addValueEventList
ener(object : ValueEventListener {
    override  fun  onDataChange(snapshot:
DataSnapshot) {
        val           tasksList          =
mutableListOf<Task>()
```

262

```kotlin
        for        (taskSnapshot        in
snapshot.children) {
            val            task            =
taskSnapshot.getValue(Task::class.java)
                task?.let { tasksList.add(it)
}
        }
        // Update RecyclerView with tasks
    }

    override    fun    onCancelled(error:
DatabaseError) {
        Log.e("Firebase",            "Error
retrieving data: ${error.message}")
    }
})
```

- o **addValueEventListener()** listens for changes to the database and updates the UI automatically with the new data.

Key Takeaways

- **Firebase Authentication**: Firebase makes it easy to implement user authentication using various sign-in methods like email/password, Google, Facebook, and more.

263

- **Realtime Database**: You can store and retrieve data in Firebase's Realtime Database using simple read and write operations.
- **Firebase Integration**: Firebase provides a seamless way to add backend functionality such as authentication and data storage to your Android apps.

In the next chapter, we will continue exploring advanced Firebase features, such as **Firebase Cloud Messaging (FCM)** for push notifications and **Firebase Analytics** for tracking app usage.

CHAPTER 23

KOTLIN FOR MODERN ANDROID DEVELOPMENT: JETPACK LIBRARIES

In this chapter, we will explore **Jetpack libraries**, a set of Android libraries that help developers write high-quality, maintainable, and flexible apps. Jetpack components are designed to simplify and streamline Android development by following best practices and reducing boilerplate code. We will cover an overview of Android Jetpack, focusing on three core components: **LiveData**, **ViewModel**, and **DataBinding**. Additionally, we will introduce the **Navigation Component**, a key Jetpack library for managing app navigation.

Overview of Android Jetpack

Jetpack is a set of Android libraries, tools, and guidance designed to help developers build robust, maintainable, and performant apps. It includes components that cover a wide range of app development tasks, such as UI components, architecture, lifecycle management, background tasks, and more.

Key benefits of using Jetpack libraries include:

- **Simplified code**: Jetpack components help reduce the amount of boilerplate code, making the codebase cleaner and easier to manage.
- **Architecture**: Jetpack encourages using modern architecture patterns such as **MVVM (Model-View-ViewModel)** and **Repository Pattern**, which improve the app's scalability and testability.
- **Backward compatibility**: Jetpack libraries are backward-compatible with older Android versions, which ensures that your app works across a wide range of devices.

Working with LiveData, ViewModel, and DataBinding

Jetpack's **LiveData**, **ViewModel**, and **DataBinding** are key components for building a modern, reactive Android app architecture. These components are often used together to implement the **MVVM (Model-View-ViewModel)** architecture, which separates the UI from the business logic.

LiveData

LiveData is an observable data holder class that is lifecycle-aware. It is used to store data that is observed by the UI components (like Activities and Fragments). The key feature of LiveData is that it only updates the UI when the component is in an active lifecycle state (e.g., `onStart()`, `onResume()`).

1. **Advantages of LiveData**:
   - o **Lifecycle awareness**: LiveData automatically manages the lifecycle of observers, so you don't need to worry about memory leaks or null pointer exceptions when the lifecycle state of an activity or fragment changes.
   - o **Data observation**: LiveData allows you to observe changes to data and automatically update the UI when the data changes.

2. **Using LiveData**:
   - o LiveData is typically used in combination with **ViewModel** (discussed below) to store UI-related data.

   Example:

```kotlin
class TaskViewModel : ViewModel() {
```

```kotlin
    private      val      _tasks      =
MutableLiveData<List<Task>>()
    val tasks: LiveData<List<Task>> get()
= _tasks

    fun loadTasks() {
        // Simulate fetching tasks from a
repository
        _tasks.value = listOf(Task("Task
1"), Task("Task 2"))
    }
}
```

- o In this example, `MutableLiveData` is used to
  store and modify the list of tasks, while the public
  `LiveData` is exposed to allow UI components to
  observe changes to the data.

Observing LiveData:

```
kotlin
```

```kotlin
class              HomeFragment          :
Fragment(R.layout.fragment_home) {
    private lateinit var taskViewModel:
TaskViewModel

    override fun onViewCreated(view: View,
savedInstanceState: Bundle?) {
```

```
        super.onViewCreated(view,
savedInstanceState)

        taskViewModel               =
ViewModelProvider(this).get(TaskViewModel
::class.java)


taskViewModel.tasks.observe(viewLifecycle
Owner, Observer { tasks ->
            // Update the UI with the tasks
            recyclerView.adapter        =
TaskAdapter(tasks)
        })

        taskViewModel.loadTasks()
    }
}
```

- o **observe()** is used to listen for changes to the
  LiveData object. The UI is updated whenever the
  data changes.

ViewModel

ViewModel is a lifecycle-aware component designed to store and manage UI-related data. It survives configuration changes, such as device rotations, and helps to keep the UI data persistent. The

269

ViewModel is intended to manage UI data for activities and fragments and separate the UI logic from business logic.

1. **Advantages of ViewModel**:
   - **Survives configuration changes**: Unlike activities and fragments, ViewModel is not destroyed during configuration changes (like rotations), ensuring that the UI data is preserved.
   - **Separation of concerns**: ViewModel helps in separating the UI logic from the business logic, making the app more maintainable and testable.

2. **Using ViewModel**:
   - The **ViewModel** holds the UI-related data and prepares it for the UI layer (e.g., `Activity` or `Fragment`). It is not responsible for UI updates, but rather for managing data and business logic.

Example:

```kotlin
kotlin

class TaskViewModel : ViewModel() {
    private val _tasks =
MutableLiveData<List<Task>>()
    val tasks: LiveData<List<Task>> get()
= _tasks

    fun loadTasks() {
```

270

```
// Simulate fetching tasks
_tasks.value = listOf(Task("Task
1"), Task("Task 2"))
    }
}
```

- o **ViewModelProvider** is used to get an instance of the ViewModel, which is then used in the Fragment to observe the data.

DataBinding

DataBinding allows you to bind UI components (like `TextViews`, `Buttons`, etc.) directly to data sources in your application. With DataBinding, you can eliminate the need for writing code that manually updates the UI.

1. **Advantages of DataBinding**:
   - o **Declarative UI**: Bind UI components to data in XML, reducing the need for boilerplate code in the `Activity` or `Fragment`.
   - o **Automatic UI updates**: When the underlying data changes, the UI automatically reflects the updates without needing to manually update each component.
2. **Using DataBinding**:

- o To use DataBinding, enable it in your `build.gradle` file:

gradle

```
android {
    viewBinding {
        enabled = true
    }
}
```

- o In your layout XML, use DataBinding to bind views directly to properties in the ViewModel.

Example Layout (`fragment_home.xml`):

xml

```
<?xml version="1.0" encoding="utf-8"?>
<layout
xmlns:android="http://schemas.android.com
/apk/res/android">
    <data>
        <variable
            name="taskViewModel"

type="com.example.app.TaskViewModel" />
    </data>
```

```xml
<androidx.constraintlayout.widget.Constra
intLayout

android:layout_width="match_parent"

android:layout_height="match_parent">


<androidx.recyclerview.widget.RecyclerVie
w

android:id="@+id/recyclerViewTasks"

android:layout_width="match_parent"

android:layout_height="match_parent"

android:adapter="@{taskViewModel.tasks}"
/>

</androidx.constraintlayout.widget.Constr
aintLayout>
</layout>
```

o With this binding setup, the RecyclerView will automatically observe the LiveData provided by the ViewModel and update the UI whenever the task data changes.

Introduction to Navigation Components

The **Navigation Component** is a Jetpack library that helps manage app navigation, including handling fragment transactions, deep links, and passing data between destinations (activities or fragments). It simplifies the process of navigating between screens and makes your app's flow easier to manage.

1. **Setting Up Navigation Component**:
   - To use the Navigation Component, first add the necessary dependencies to your `build.gradle` file:

```gradle
dependencies {
    implementation
'androidx.navigation:navigation-
fragment-ktx:2.3.5'
    implementation
'androidx.navigation:navigation-ui-
ktx:2.3.5'
}
```

2. **Creating a Navigation Graph**:
   - A **navigation graph** is an XML file that defines all the possible destinations (fragments and

activities) and the actions between them. It helps organize the app's navigation in a centralized way.

Example (nav_graph.xml):

xml

```
<navigation
xmlns:android="http://schemas.android.com/apk/res/android"
    android:id="@+id/nav_graph"

app:startDestination="@id/homeFragment">

    <fragment
        android:id="@+id/homeFragment"

android:name="com.example.app.HomeFragment"
        android:label="Home"

app:destination="@id/taskDetailFragment"
/>

    <fragment

android:id="@+id/taskDetailFragment"
```

275

```
android:name="com.example.app.TaskDetailF
ragment"
        android:label="Task Detail" />
</navigation>
```

3. **Navigating Between Fragments**:
   - You can navigate between destinations using the NavController. You can use actions defined in the navigation graph or manually call navigate() to move between fragments.

   Example (Navigating from HomeFragment to TaskDetailFragment):

   ```kotlin
   kotlin

   val             action             =
   HomeFragmentDirections.actionHomeFragment
   ToTaskDetailFragment(taskId)
   findNavController().navigate(action)
   ```

   - **Safe Args**: You can use **Safe Args** to pass data between destinations in a type-safe manner. This prevents errors related to incorrect argument types.

4. **Handling the Up Button**:
   - The Navigation Component automatically handles the **Up Button** (back navigation) and

276

provides methods to control it. You don't need to manually manage back stack operations.

```kotlin
val            navController            =
findNavController(R.id.nav_host_fragment)
setupActionBarWithNavController(navContro
ller)
```

- o The
  setupActionBarWithNavController()
  method automatically configures the up button to navigate to the previous fragment.

Key Takeaways

- **Jetpack Libraries**: Jetpack libraries, including **LiveData**, **ViewModel**, **DataBinding**, and **Navigation**, simplify Android development and promote modern app architecture practices like MVVM.
- **LiveData**: LiveData is a lifecycle-aware data holder class that allows you to observe data changes and update the UI accordingly.

- **ViewModel**: ViewModel helps manage and store UI-related data and survives configuration changes, ensuring that the UI data is preserved even after device rotations.
- **DataBinding**: DataBinding allows you to bind UI components to data sources, reducing boilerplate code and automatically updating the UI when data changes.
- **Navigation Component**: The Navigation Component simplifies navigating between fragments, passing data, and managing the app's navigation flow.

In the next chapter, we will explore how to implement advanced features such as **background tasks**, **push notifications**, and **performance optimization** in your Android app using Jetpack libraries and Firebase.

CHAPTER 24

ADVANCED KOTLIN FEATURES

In this chapter, we will explore some of the more advanced features of Kotlin that can help improve the functionality, readability, and maintainability of your Android applications. These features include **extension functions**, **sealed classes**, **data classes**, **delegation**, and **reflection**. By understanding and utilizing these features, you can write cleaner, more efficient, and more flexible Kotlin code.

Extension Functions

Extension functions allow you to add new functionality to existing classes without modifying their source code. This feature is particularly useful when you want to extend the functionality of a class without creating a subclass.

1. **How Extension Functions Work**:
   - Extension functions are defined outside of the class they are extending but can be called as if they were a member of that class.

279

- o They allow you to add functionality to existing types like `String`, `Int`, or even your own classes.

2. **Creating Extension Functions**: To define an extension function, you simply declare it with the type you want to extend followed by the function name.

Example (Extension function for the `String` class):

kotlin

```
fun    String.addPrefix(prefix:    String):
String {
    return prefix + this
}
```

- o This function adds a prefix to a string. The function is defined as an extension of the `String` class.

3. **Using Extension Functions**: Once defined, you can call the extension function on any instance of the class it extends.

Example:

kotlin

```
val result = "Kotlin".addPrefix("Hello, ")
println(result)  // Output: "Hello, Kotlin"
```

4. **Extension Function on Custom Classes**: You can also define extension functions for your own classes to add utility methods.

Example (Extension function for a custom class):

```kotlin
kotlin

data class User(val name: String, val age: Int)

fun User.isAdult(): Boolean {
    return age >= 18
}

val user = User("John", 25)
println(user.isAdult())  // Output: true
```

Sealed Classes and Data Classes

Kotlin provides **sealed classes** and **data classes** to make your code more expressive, concise, and easier to manage.

Sealed Classes

A **sealed class** is a special class in Kotlin that restricts class hierarchies. You can define a limited set of subclasses for a sealed class, which makes it easier to handle when working with patterns like when expressions.

1. **Why Use Sealed Classes**: Sealed classes are useful when you want to represent a restricted class hierarchy and ensure that all possible subclasses are known at compile time.

2. **Creating a Sealed Class**: Sealed classes are declared using the sealed keyword and can have subclasses, but all subclasses must be declared within the same file.

Example:

```kotlin

sealed class Result

data class Success(val message: String) : Result()
data class Error(val error: String) : Result()
object Loading : Result()
```

3. **Using Sealed Classes**: You can use a sealed class with a when expression to handle the different types of results.

Example:

```kotlin
```

```
fun handleResult(result: Result) {
    when (result) {
        is Success -> println("Success:
${result.message}")
        is Error -> println("Error:
${result.error}")
        is Loading ->
println("Loading...")
    }
}
```

- o This ensures that all subclasses of the sealed class are handled, and the compiler will warn you if a subclass is missing from the `when` expression.

Data Classes

A **data class** in Kotlin is a class that is primarily used to hold data. It automatically generates useful methods like `toString()`, `equals()`, `hashCode()`, and `()`.

1. **Why Use Data Classes**: Data classes are great for models or objects that just hold data and don't require additional behavior. Kotlin automatically generates the necessary methods for you, which reduces boilerplate code.

2. **Creating a Data Class**: You define a data class using the `data` keyword, followed by the class definition.

Example:

```kotlin
data class User(val name: String, val age: Int)
```

3. **Using Data Classes**: The compiler automatically provides implementations for methods like `toString()`, `equals()`, and `()`.

Example:

```kotlin
val user1 = User("Alice", 25)
val user2 = User("Alice", 25)

println(user1)            //       Output: User(name=Alice, age=25)
println(user1 == user2)   // Output: true

// ing a data class object
val user3 = user1.(name = "Bob")
println(user3)   // Output: User(name=Bob, age=25)
```

- (): A special method for creating a of a data class object with some properties changed.

- o **toString()**: Provides a readable string representation of the data class.

- o **equals()** and **hashCode()**: These are automatically implemented for data classes based on their properties.

Delegation and Reflection in Kotlin

Delegation

Delegation is a design pattern where an object relies on another object to perform some task on its behalf. Kotlin makes it easy to implement delegation with the by keyword.

1. **Standard Delegation**: Kotlin has built-in support for standard delegation. You can delegate the implementation of an interface to another object.

Example:

```kotlin
kotlin

interface Printer {
    fun print()
}

class ConsolePrinter : Printer {
    override fun print() {
```

```kotlin
        println("Printing       to       the
console...")
    }
}

class DelegatingPrinter(printer: Printer)
: Printer by printer

val consolePrinter = ConsolePrinter()
val          delegatingPrinter          =
DelegatingPrinter(consolePrinter)
delegatingPrinter.print()      // Output:
Printing to the console...
```

2. **Lazy Delegation**: Kotlin also provides a built-in delegation for **lazy initialization** with the `lazy` function. This ensures that a value is only computed when it's first accessed.

Example:

```kotlin
kotlin

val lazyValue: String by lazy {
    println("Initializing value")
    "Hello, Kotlin"
}
```

286

```
println(lazyValue)              //      Output:
Initializing value \n Hello, Kotlin
```

- o The `lazy` delegate ensures that the initialization code is run only when `lazyValue` is accessed for the first time.

Reflection

Reflection in Kotlin allows you to inspect and manipulate objects at runtime. You can access class metadata, properties, functions, and even modify them dynamically.

1. **Accessing Class Information**: You can use **reflection** to get details about a class, such as its name, methods, and properties.

   Example:

   ```kotlin
   data class User(val name: String, val age: Int)

   val user = User("Alice", 25)
   val userClass = user::class

   println(userClass.simpleName)  // Output: User
   ```

```
println(userClass.members)        // Output:
[public abstract val name: kotlin.String,
...]
```

2. **Calling Methods Using Reflection**: You can call methods dynamically at runtime using reflection.

   Example:

   ```kotlin
   val method = user::class.members.find {
   it.name == "" }
   val copiedUser = method?.call(user, name =
   "Bob")
   println(copiedUser)              //      Output:
   User(name=Bob, age=25)
   ```

3. **Reflection for Property Access**: Kotlin's reflection library allows you to access and modify properties of an object.

   Example:

   ```kotlin
   val            nameProperty        =
   user::class.members.find  {  it.name  ==
   "name" }
   ```

```
println(nameProperty?.call(user))        //
Output: Alice
```

Key Takeaways

- **Extension Functions**: Allow you to add functionality to existing classes without modifying their code, making your code more flexible and reusable.
- **Sealed Classes**: Provide a way to represent restricted class hierarchies, which are useful for modeling states, responses, or events with a limited set of possibilities.
- **Data Classes**: Automatically generate methods like `toString()`, `equals()`, and `()` for classes that are used to hold data, reducing boilerplate code.
- **Delegation**: A powerful pattern in Kotlin that is simplified with the `by` keyword, allowing you to delegate functionality to another object or property.
- **Reflection**: Provides runtime introspection, enabling you to inspect classes, functions, and properties dynamically.

By mastering these advanced Kotlin features, you can write more concise, efficient, and maintainable code, making your Android applications more flexible and robust. In the next chapter, we will explore **Kotlin Coroutines** in more depth, which is a vital feature for handling background tasks and asynchronous programming in Android.

CHAPTER 25

APP PERFORMANCE AND OPTIMIZATION

In this chapter, we will focus on optimizing the performance of your Android app, covering key areas such as **layout rendering**, **memory management**, and strategies for **improving app startup time** and **reducing APK size**. These optimizations are critical for providing a smooth, responsive user experience, especially when dealing with large or complex apps.

Optimizing Layout Rendering

One of the most common performance bottlenecks in Android apps is inefficient layout rendering. Inefficient layouts can lead to **janky scrolling**, **slow UI rendering**, and **increased battery consumption**. Here's how you can optimize layout rendering:

1. **Use ConstraintLayout**: **ConstraintLayout** is a flexible, performant layout that can replace nested layouts (e.g., `LinearLayout`, `RelativeLayout`) in many cases. It reduces the number of layout passes required to position views, leading to improved performance.

- o **Advantages**: `ConstraintLayout` flattens view hierarchies and reduces the number of view groups that need to be laid out. It also supports more complex layouts without nesting.

Example:

xml

```
<androidx.constraintlayout.widget.Constra
intLayout
xmlns:android="http://schemas.android.com
/apk/res/android"
    android:layout_width="match_parent"
    android:layout_height="match_parent">

    <TextView
        android:id="@+id/textView"

android:layout_width="wrap_content"

android:layout_height="wrap_content"
        android:text="Hello World!"

app:layout_constraintTop_toTopOf="parent"

app:layout_constraintStart_toStartOf="par
ent" />
```

```
</androidx.constraintlayout.widget.Constr
aintLayout>
```

- o Use **ConstraintLayout** to reduce layout nesting and improve rendering performance.

2. **Avoid Overdraw**: **Overdraw** occurs when the system draws pixels multiple times for the same screen area, which can slow down rendering. To avoid this:
   - o Use **alpha** transparency sparingly, as it requires additional GPU resources.
   - o Check the **GPU Rendering** in **Developer Options** to visualize overdraw (red areas indicate overdraw).

Best Practice:

- o Minimize the number of layers and use **solid background colors** rather than transparent backgrounds.

3. **Use ViewStub for Lazy Layout Inflation**: A **ViewStub** is a lightweight view that only inflates the layout when it's needed. This is particularly useful for complex UI sections that aren't immediately visible (e.g., expanding panels, lazy loading content).

Example:

```
xml
```

```
<ViewStub

    android:id="@+id/viewStub"

    android:layout_width="match_parent"

    android:layout_height="wrap_content"

android:inflatedId="@+id/expandedView"

android:layout="@layout/expanded_layout"
/>
```

- o **ViewStub** allows you to defer the inflation of complex layouts until they are actually needed, improving the initial rendering performance.

4. **Use RecyclerView for Lists**: For displaying long lists of data, always use **RecyclerView** instead of `ListView`. `RecyclerView` is optimized for performance and memory usage, as it reuses item views that are no longer visible, rather than creating new ones every time.

   - o Use **ViewHolder** and **LayoutManager** to optimize view reuse and smooth scrolling.

Example:

```kotlin
```

```
val      recyclerView:      RecyclerView    =
findViewById(R.id.recyclerView)
recyclerView.layoutManager                  =
LinearLayoutManager(this)
recyclerView.adapter = MyAdapter(data)
```

Memory Management in Android Apps

Memory management is essential for ensuring that your app runs efficiently and does not consume unnecessary resources. Android provides several tools and techniques for managing memory effectively:

1. **Avoid Memory Leaks**: A **memory leak** occurs when objects are not properly released and continue to occupy memory even when they are no longer needed. Common sources of memory leaks in Android apps include:

    o **Context**: Storing a reference to an `Activity` or `Context` object that outlives its lifecycle.

    o **Static references**: Using static references to hold onto objects that should be garbage collected.

    Best Practice:

    o Use **WeakReference** when holding references to `Context` or other objects that should not prevent garbage collection.

294

2. **Use `Android Profiler` for Memory Monitoring**: Android Studio provides the **Android Profiler** tool to monitor your app's memory usage in real-time. You can use it to identify memory leaks, excessive memory usage, or objects that are not being properly released.

   o **Heap Dump**: Take a heap dump to analyze the objects in memory and track down memory leaks.

   o **Allocation Tracker**: Track object allocations to identify inefficient code that creates too many objects.

3. **Optimize Bitmaps and Images**: **Images** are often the largest consumers of memory in an Android app. Large, unoptimized bitmaps can lead to **OutOfMemoryError** crashes and excessive memory usage.

   o Use **`BitmapFactory`** and the **`inSampleSize`** option to load scaled-down versions of images.

   o Use **`Glide`** or **`Picasso`** libraries to efficiently load and cache images in the background.

Example (Loading a scaled image):

```kotlin
val options = BitmapFactory.Options()
options.inSampleSize = 2   // Reduce the
size by a factor of 2
```

295

```
val              bitmap              =
BitmapFactory.decodeResource(resources,
R.drawable.image, options)
```

4. **Release Resources When Not Needed**:
   o Close resources like **Cursor**, **File**, and **Streams** when done to release system resources.
   o Use **onDestroy()** or **onStop()** to clean up resources in your Activities and Fragments.

Improving App Startup Time and Reducing APK Size

App startup time is a crucial factor in user experience. Slow startups can frustrate users and lead to high app abandonment rates. Similarly, a large APK size can negatively impact download times and storage usage.

1. **Optimizing App Startup Time**: The key to improving startup time is to minimize the number of operations performed during app launch and defer unnecessary tasks.
   o **Lazy Loading**: Load non-critical resources only when needed. Use **Lazy Initialization** for resources like images, data, or fragments that aren't essential for the initial screen.

o **Profile Your Startup Time**: Use **Android Profiler** to analyze how long the app takes to start and identify any bottlenecks.

Best Practice:

o Defer initialization tasks, such as loading large data sets or making network requests, until after the main UI is visible.

2. **Reducing APK Size**: Large APKs increase the time it takes for users to download the app, as well as use up more device storage. Here are strategies to reduce APK size:

o **Use ProGuard or R8**: These tools optimize the code by removing unused code, shrinking the APK, and obfuscating the code to protect intellectual property.

Example (Enable ProGuard in `build.gradle`):

```gradle
gradle

buildTypes {
    release {
        minifyEnabled    true       //
Enable code shrinking
        shrinkResources   true      //
Remove unused resources
```

```
       proguardFiles
getDefaultProguardFile('proguard-
android-optimize.txt'),   'proguard-
rules.pro'
    }
}
```

- o **Remove Unused Resources**: Use `lint` or Android Studio's **"Unused Resources"** tool to identify and remove unused images, layouts, and other resources.
- o **Use App Bundles**: Instead of delivering a single APK, use **Android App Bundles** to serve optimized APKs for different devices. This reduces the APK size by only delivering the resources and code necessary for each device configuration.

Example (Using Android App Bundles):

```
gradle
```

```
android {
    bundle {
        language {
            enableSplit = true
        }
    }
}
```

298

3. **Optimize Third-Party Libraries**:

   o Only include libraries that are essential for your app. Avoid adding large libraries if only a small part of the library is used.

   o Consider using the **Android Jetpack libraries** for common functionality instead of large external libraries.

4. **Optimize Images and Assets**:

   o Compress images using formats like **WebP** instead of PNG or JPEG, as WebP offers better compression and quality.

   o Use **Vector Drawables** where possible instead of image assets to reduce the size of the APK.

Key Takeaways

- **Layout Rendering Optimization**: Use `ConstraintLayout` to reduce view hierarchy complexity, avoid overdraw, and utilize `ViewStub` for lazy layout inflation. Use `RecyclerView` for efficient list rendering.

- **Memory Management**: Avoid memory leaks by managing references properly, using tools like **Android Profiler** to monitor memory usage, and optimizing image loading.

- **Improving Startup Time**: Use lazy loading, defer non-essential tasks, and profile app startup time to identify bottlenecks.

- **Reducing APK Size**: Use ProGuard/R8 for code shrinking and obfuscation, remove unused resources, and consider using **Android App Bundles** for optimized APKs for different devices.

By focusing on these optimizations, you can build Android apps that perform better, have faster startup times, and are more efficient in terms of memory and storage usage.

CHAPTER 26

PUBLISHING YOUR ANDROID APP

In this final chapter, we'll walk you through the process of publishing your Android app. This includes preparing your app for release, signing your APK or AAB, uploading it to the **Google Play Store**, and managing post-release updates and maintenance. Publishing your app is a critical step to getting your work out there and into the hands of users, and it's essential to follow the right process to ensure your app is successful.

Preparing for Release

Before you publish your app, you need to ensure that it's fully prepared for production. This means optimizing your app, testing it thoroughly, and making sure that it meets all the necessary requirements for release.

1. **Final Testing**:
    o   Perform **final tests** on your app to make sure it works correctly on all supported devices and screen sizes. Ensure that you have tested the app on both emulators and real devices.

- o **Test app performance** to ensure it runs smoothly, with no crashes or slowdowns, and that it uses minimal resources (e.g., memory and CPU).
- o **Test edge cases**: Check how your app behaves with unexpected inputs or in low-network conditions.

2. **Remove Debugging Code**:
   - o Ensure that any **debugging code** (e.g., logs, test configurations) is removed from the app before the final build. You should only include essential features and release-specific code in your final version.

Example:

- o Remove all `Log.d()` statements or replace them with appropriate release-level logging.

3. **Update App Version**:
   - o Make sure you update the **version code** and **version name** in your `build.gradle` file for proper version management.

Example:

```gradle
android {
```

```
defaultConfig {
    versionCode  2    //  Incremented
version code
    versionName  "1.1"   //  Updated
version name
  }
}
```

- o **versionCode** is an integer value that must increase with each release to the Google Play Store. **versionName** is a string that represents the version of the app shown to users.

4. **Review Permissions**:
   - o Review the **permissions** your app is requesting. Make sure they are necessary for the app's functionality, and remove any unnecessary permissions. Google Play may reject your app if it requests sensitive permissions without justification.

Signing Your APK or AAB

To release your Android app, you need to sign it with a **release key** to ensure the authenticity and integrity of the app. This process is required by Android for all apps that are published on the Google Play Store.

1. **Generate a Keystore File**: If you haven't already, you will need to generate a **keystore** file to sign your APK or AAB. A keystore is a binary file that contains one or more private keys used to sign your app.

   o Use Android Studio's **Build** menu to generate a signed APK/AAB, or you can manually create a keystore file using the **keytool** command.

   Example (Using `keytool` to create a keystore):

   bash

   ```
   keytool -genkeypair -v -keystore my-
   release-key.keystore -keyalg RSA -keysize
   2048 -validity 10000 -dname "CN=MyApp,
   OU=Dev, O=MyCompany, L=City, ST=State,
   C=Country"
   ```

   This will generate a keystore file `my-release-key.keystore` that you can use for signing your APK/AAB.

2. **Sign the APK or AAB**:
   o After you've generated the keystore file, you can sign your app in **Android Studio** by going to **Build > Generate Signed Bundle/APK**.
   o Select either **APK** or **Android App Bundle (AAB)** as the build type. Google Play now

recommends uploading an **AAB** instead of an APK, as it's optimized for delivery to users.

Steps to Sign APK or AAB:

o   Choose **Build > Generate Signed APK/AAB**.
o   Select **Release** as the build variant.
o   Provide the keystore details: keystore file path, key alias, and key password.
o   Build the APK or AAB.

Example:

o   For **APK**, you'll generate a signed APK that's ready for release.
o   For **AAB**, you'll create an Android App Bundle that will be uploaded to the Google Play Console.

Uploading to the Google Play Store

Once your app is signed and ready for release, you can upload it to the **Google Play Store**. This process involves several steps:

1. **Create a Google Play Developer Account**:
    o   If you haven't already, you will need to create a **Google Play Developer Account**. This requires a one-time fee of $25 USD.

o   Sign up at the Google Play Console.

2. **Prepare Store Listing**: In the Google Play Console, you will need to prepare your **store listing**. This includes:

- o   **App Name**: A unique name for your app.

- o   **App Description**: A clear and concise description of your app's features.

- o   **Screenshots**: Provide at least 2-3 screenshots of your app (on different devices like phones and tablets).

- o   **App Category**: Choose an appropriate category for your app (e.g., Games, Productivity, etc.).

- o   **App Icon**: Upload a high-quality, 512x512 px icon for your app.

- o   **Privacy Policy**: If your app collects any user data, you must include a privacy policy link.

3. **Upload the APK or AAB**:

- o   In the **Google Play Console**, go to your app's **Release** section.

- o   Click on **Create Release**.

- o   You can either upload the APK or AAB file you've generated.

- o   Fill in any release notes (what's new in this version).

After uploading the APK or AAB, Google Play will run a verification process to check for any issues with your app.

4. **Set Pricing and Distribution**:

   o **Pricing**: You can choose whether your app will be **free** or **paid**. Note that once you choose to make an app free, you cannot change it to paid.

   o **Distribution**: Choose the countries where you want your app to be available. You can select **global distribution** or limit your app to specific regions.

5. **Submit for Review**: After filling out all the required information and uploading the APK/AAB, click **Review and Rollout**. Google will then review your app and notify you if there are any issues. This can take several hours to a few days.

Post-Release Management and Updates

Once your app is live, the work doesn't end there. Regular updates, bug fixes, and performance improvements are essential to maintaining a positive user experience and keeping your app competitive.

1. **Monitor App Performance**:

   o Use **Google Play Console** to monitor key metrics such as **crash reports**, **user ratings**, and **app installs**.

- o Integrate **Firebase Analytics** and **Crashlytics** to get real-time insights into how users are interacting with your app and identify any issues.

2. **Respond to User Feedback**:
   - o Regularly check user feedback and ratings in the **Google Play Console**.
   - o Respond to user comments to show that you care about their feedback. Address bugs and suggestions promptly.
   - o **Improve the app** by updating it frequently based on user feedback to fix bugs or add requested features.

3. **App Updates**:
   - o As you release new versions of your app, make sure to increment the **version code** and **version name** in the `build.gradle` file before signing and uploading the new APK or AAB.
   - o Provide **release notes** with each update to explain what's new or fixed.
   - o You can upload a new version by following the same steps as the initial upload process, but selecting **"Update"** instead of **"Create Release"**.

4. **Monitor App Performance Over Time**:
   - o **Google Play Console** provides performance reports, user acquisition data, and crash reports

that help you assess your app's performance and identify areas for improvement.

○ Use tools like **Firebase Performance Monitoring** and **Firebase Crashlytics** for advanced tracking.

Key Takeaways

- **Preparing for Release**: Test your app thoroughly, remove debugging code, and update version codes before the release.

- **Signing APK or AAB**: Sign your app using a release key to ensure security and integrity. Use an **AAB** for optimized distribution.

- **Uploading to Google Play**: Create a developer account, prepare your store listing, upload the signed APK or AAB, and configure pricing and distribution.

- **Post-Release Management**: Monitor your app's performance through Google Play Console and Firebase, respond to user feedback, and release regular updates to keep the app fresh and bug-free.

By following these steps, you will be able to successfully publish your app and manage it efficiently post-release.

www.ingramcontent.com/pod-product-compliance
Lightning Source LLC
LaVergne TN
LVHW051433050326
832903LV00030BD/3062